Angel in the Kitchen 2

୬୭✖୧ଚ

A Second Helping of Wit & Wisdom Inspired by Food, Cooking, Kitchen Tools and Appliances!

Angel in the Kitchen 2

❦

A Second Helping of Wit & Wisdom Inspired by Food, Cooking, Kitchen Tools and Appliances!

Wilma Espaillat English And Tom English

RAVENS'
READS
AN IMPRINT OF **DEAD LETTER PRESS**
BOX 134, NEW KENT, VA 23124-0134

Angel in the Kitchen 2
First published 2021 by Ravens' Reads
An imprint of
DEAD LETTER PRESS

The articles collected in *Angel in the Kitchen 2* originally appeared on the website www.AngelattheDoor.com, and were revised for this edition.

Printed in the United States of America

ISBN-13: 978-1-7324344-7-9

FIRST EDITION
January 2021

DEAD LETTER PRESS
BOX 134, NEW KENT, VIRGINIA 23124-0134

*This book is
lovingly dedicated to*

Tía (Aunt) Gladys

and

Tío (Uncle) José

For their prayers and hospitality.

CONTENTS:

Cooking Up a Second Serving of Wit & Wisdom!

For the invisible things of [God],
His eternal power and divinity,
are clearly understood by the creation
of the world and by the things that are made....
—Romans 1:20 JUB

IN OUR FIRST VOLUME in the series *Angel in the Kitchen,* we introduced our readers to some of the "angels" in our kitchen: a gang of eccentric gadgets and appliances that continues to teach us with wit and wisdom many of the most important lessons about life, love, relationships, and the nature of our loving and hospitable God. Among these wide-ranging teachings employing food and cooking, we wrote about our twin microwave ovens, Luke and Nuke; about the call of the Keurig; and why Fridgey (our refrigerator) enjoys the nightlife. We discussed God and groceries, crock pot promises and microwave mentality, the spiritual significance of Tupperware, and what happens when "The Cheese Stands Alone"—and we had a blast doing it. *No one is as creative as our Lord, the Master Chef!*

Back by popular demand, these kitchen angels are ready to serve up a second helping of their inspiring and

1

encouraging adventures that will leave you thinking and laughing long after you've finished this book. For we have found that many of the common sights and practices found daily in the average kitchen are analogous to an incredible wealth of Biblical insights: cooking techniques, such as simmering and microwaving; natural and processed foods, such as eggs and onions, canned goods and boxed items; gadgets such as blenders and coffeemakers; not to mention those "talkative" appliances. Basically, every *thing*—actually, every *one*—has a special, anointed message to deliver.

And why not? In the Bible, God has an army of heavenly messengers called *angels*, and ocassionally these supernatural beings visited earth in the guise of travelers on the byways of life. But in a manner of speaking, *anything* God uses to speak to us, becomes His "messenger." In this sense, God's "angels" can visit us in a variety of forms. We can acquire truth from the Bible, as well as from our spiritual leaders; and even from books, music, television and movies.

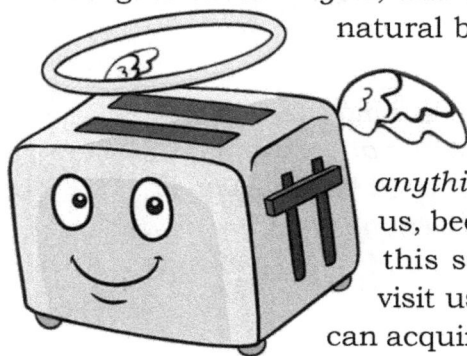

We can hear God speak to us in the roar of the ocean surf, see His wisdom in a blade of grass, and learn important lessons from industrious ants and puffy rain clouds. If we're attuned to what God is trying to teach us, we soon realize that every creation in nature, including the people in our lives, and *really*, every thing in life itself, has a special message to impart—an *angelic* role to play.

Most of our readers know by now that we enjoy naming our kitchen appliances. If we had a lot of money, we'd be called eccentric—but we don't, so just call us looney. But honestly, sometimes we think those inanimate kitchen objects are ... well, more *animated* than a few people we know. Our appliances play a big part in our interactions in the kitchen, and we've come to view them as faithful friends and allies in our culinary misadventures. And, through their various mechanical traits and duties, these little guys continue to inspire us with many amazing life lessons. Read on, and you'll understand why we've grown so fond of these "angels in the kitchen."

Presented here for your enjoyment are over five dozen of the best articles from our web-series *Angel in the Kitchen*. We hope you'll relish this second serving of tasty nuggets of wit and wisdom as much as we enjoyed relating them. *Bon appétit!*

Wilma Espaillat English
Tom English
New Kent, VA

Tom and Wilma English invite you to join them each weekday at their internet home, **AngelAtTheDoor.com**, for humorous and inspiring articles presented in three rotating series:

Diet for Dreamers
Angel in the Kitchen
Encouragement for Creators

Grounds for Offense

FOR SOME TIME NOW, we have faithfully related all of the wit and wisdom we've gleaned from the eccentric collection of kitchen tools and appliances inhabiting our humble home. Each of these "kitchen angels" has a unique message to announce—about life, love and relationships! We need only "listen" for it. For instance, while dicing onions, Mack the Knife taught us the importance of knowing what we're cut out for in this wonderful world; and the onion ... as we tearfully chopped the poor guy to pieces ... gave us new insights into human relationships. No, *really!*[1]

Comrade Keurig, who daily brews delicious mugs of coffee while *shooshing, sighing,* and *flashing* friendly little messages, shared with us the benefits of finding your own unique voice, and ... well, the list goes on. Speaking of Comrade Keurig, a relative newcomer to our kitchen, it's high time we introduced another, older member of the family—one who's been with us for many years, a veteran of countless culinary campaigns, who's valiantly served us ... coffee by the potful!

He's generally unassuming and soft-spoken, the strong silent type. You know, more a gadget of deeds than words. But now he wants his "say"! Not to worry, however, because given the very nature of this guy, he'll never blurt

---

[1] Both lessons are featured in *Angel in the Kitchen,* the first book in this series.

out anything inappropriate. Of this we're certain, and we'll explain why. But first, *heeeere's Mister Coffee!*

Hey, tough guy. Take a bow while we discuss your sterling character!

Mister Coffee is in the Kitchen Angel Reserves. We only call upon his services for those really big jobs that Mr. Keurig can't handle all by himself. Now, we're not minimizing the efforts of Comrade Keurig; after all, he's the fastest java brewer on the block. (*Shh!* Please don't let him know that we live in the woods and our nearest neighbor is a five-minute walk down the lane!) And he can brew a cup of hazelnut coffee in one minute, and a cup of mocha the very next! But sometimes, when we're hosting many guests, we need volume more than variety.

Never fear, Mister Coffee's here! He can produce up to twelve cups of joe faster than we can ask our numerous guests, "Cream and sugar?" And his potent brew is always delicious—except for one occasion when we forgot to insert his special paper filter. Because Mister Coffee's filter wasn't in place, we got a nasty-looking sludge that was part coffee and part disgusting grounds! True, there *was* a form of coffee present in this thick black liquid; but no one would be able to benefit from it, because of the nasty, bitter grounds that were present. Anyone attempting to drink this noxious brew would have choked on it!

Mister Coffee gazed up at us from his spot on the kitchen counter, and sighed in exasperation. We knew exactly what he was trying to communicate: his filter absolutely must be in place, or what comes through will not be palatable! No matter how fresh the blend, no matter how stimulating the brew, if the stuff isn't properly filtered, then no one will benefit from it. In fact, anyone consuming it will probably get sick!

This truth applies not just to Mister Coffee, but also to each and every one of us. In life, we often hear statements like "She has no filter to her brain" or "He'd do well to filter his words." We usually get such pronouncements right after someone makes a comment that is hurtful or embarrassing. Young children, for instance, don't seem to develop a filter until much later, and are prone to say things which would make their parents blush. Quite forgivable, though, because they don't know any better. But we do. So, parents should teach their children that some questions are too personal, and some observations are too embarrassing —or just plain inappropriate. Learning to develop a "filter" is part of the maturing process.

In a spiritual sense, our Heavenly Father desires that we, too, grow up and develop a "filter." He wants us to apply a Godly characteristic to filter our words and deeds, while blocking the wrongful attitudes and actions that can leave people with a bitter taste. What is this filter? The Apostle Paul states, "...Speak the truth in love, growing in every way more and more like Christ...." (Ephesians 4:15 NLT).

Having the filter of love properly in place will keep us from blurting out the first thing that pops into our heads, which is usually the wrong thing to say. The filter of love will ensure that our conversation is always refreshing to those who hear it—that our words are potent but palatable, beneficial and not bitter, invigorating and not insulting. In fact, without the filter of love, our speech is a lot like what Mister Coffee brewed up the day we forgot his filter: a noxious and obnoxious blend of nastiness that benefits no one.

But don't take our word for it! The Bible states, "[If I] could speak in every language there is in all of heaven and earth, but didn't love others, I would only be making noise." (1 Corinthians 13:1 TLB) *Noise* is defined as harsh, unpleasant, and unwanted sounds; and the term comes from the same Latin root word for *nausea*. Yes, without love to remove the bitter "grounds," we can indeed sicken people with our speech.

So, when conversing with your spouse, or a child, or a friend, or a coworker, make sure your love filter is in place! And whenever you're about to confront anyone regarding an issue or a problem that's affecting you or someone you care about—whether in the area of human relationships, a job, a faith community, or life in general—please pray first! Ask God to help you speak the truth in love; to remove any feelings of resentment, self-righteousness or selfish motives; and to filter out any hateful, arrogant, or demeaning words. Don't give those around you "grounds for offense": more bitterness, more discontentment, more prejudice, more division (including separation and divorce); or an easy excuse to ignore what you have to say. And please apply this filter when using social media, too.

"Love is patient [and] kind. It does not envy, it does not boast, it is not proud. It does not dishonor others, it is not self-seeking, it is not easily angered, it keeps no record of wrongs. ...It always protects, always trusts, always hopes, always perseveres...." (1 Corinthians 13:4-7 NIV)

A Cereal Crime

HAVE YOU BEEN THE VICTIM of a cereal crime?

Not *serial*, but cereal—as in a breakfast food produced from roasted grain. Although "serial" *does* denote an act or behavior committed repeatedly, at regular intervals, and sometimes even compulsively; which pretty much describes

our breakfast habits, such as eating cereal. And not *really* a "crime" as in a wanton and often calculated violation of legislated laws; but rather something we consider a deplorable practice (as in, "Shame on you!") born out of wanton greed and/or calculated (planned) results. Confused? You should be. So, let's settle our brains with a bit of background.

Breakfast cereal was created, quite by accident, in 1898. At the time, Dr. John Kellogg was operating a sanitarium in Battle Creek, Michigan. After his brother Will arrived to help run things, the two men decided to whip up a nutritious batch of granola (using wheat berry) to feed their "patients." Although the brothers failed miserably at preparing granola, they accidentally hit upon a method for creating wheat flakes, thereby forever changing the course of culinary history. Dare we state it? The first *flake* was a *fluke!*

Will Kellogg continued tinkering in the kitchen, using other grains, and eventually created corn flakes. He told his brother, the good doctor, to keep the recipe a secret. But John was so proud of the process used to create the flakes, that he couldn't resist demonstrating it to one of his patients, a businessman named Post. Big mistake. C. W. Post immediately implemented the new process in the manufacture of his own Post Cereals, thus getting the jump on the brothers Kellogg, and ultimately becoming their greatest competitor. Apparently, the early bird gets far more for breakfast than just the worm.

We stated that Post was a "patient" at Dr. Kellogg's sanitarium. Allow us to explain. In this case, the sanitarium was sort of like a club for health nuts. Not to be confused with a *sanatorium*—which is sort of like a club for ... the mentally ill. (We'd write "nuts" again, just to underscore the analogy, but that would be in very bad taste.) So ... at Kellogg's *sanitarium* a doctor created a bunch of flakes. But at a *sanatorium* doctors *treat* a bunch of flakes! (*Cough. Totally inexcusable.*)

After his brother divulged the secret for a smart breakfast, W. K. Kellogg left the sanitarium in a huff. In 1906, he started up the Battle Creek Toasted Corn Flake Company, hired 44 employees, and created the first commercial batch of the breakfast cereal that would eventually be called *Kellogg's Corn Flakes.*

But what's all this about a "cereal crime"? Well, have you ever opened a new box of your favorite breakfast cereal and—*surprise!*—wondered why the package looks only "half full"? (Or, depending upon your general outlook, "half *empty.*") You go to the market, grab the biggest container of cereal you can find, perhaps one of those cheaper, store brands packaged in a box the size of a steamer trunk, take it home, and ... *Hey, dude, where'd my cereal go?*

Feel cheated?

If you turn the box over you should be able to find the typical rationale: "Some settling may occur."

What the manufacturer is trying to say is this: *We filled this box to the brim with good stuff. Honest. But afterward the stuff got all shaken together, and it settled. But, trust us, it's still a full box.*

Really? A full box? It doesn't *look* full. "Full" is *full,* practically half empty ain't full! And yet, the cereal company plainly states on each box that at one time it *was* full. *Sure....* But what about now? The label further states that the cereal company actually knew in advance that "some settling" would occur! For shame! Such wanton—*and calculated*—neglect. Why can't these companies fill the box, shake it down, fill it some more, let that settle, and then top it off? Imagine the joy of opening a box of Sugar-Coma Clumpies and actually finding it *full!* What a thing to behold, a box brimming with a breakfast bounty!

Yeah, we know, some things in life just can't be helped—such as the law of gravity. Still, that half-full box can give one pause to ponder the great mysteries of the Universe. And the Creator of the Universe knows this. In fact, our Heavenly Father understands our disappointment over such things. Which is why He's careful when supplying His many gifts and blessings. Especially in regards to blessing us when we donate our time, talents, and personal resources to doing God's work of helping those around us.

He will *never* give us half of anything! He fills the "cup" till it's running over—and He takes special precautions to prevent settling during "shipping."

Read the back of the "box" of God's promises (the Bible). It plainly states: "...Your gift will return to you in <u>full</u> and overflowing measure, pressed down, <u>shaken together</u> to make room for more, and <u>running over</u>. Whatever measure you use to give ... will be used to measure what is given back to you." (Luke 6:38 TLB)

Garbo's da Name,
Garbage is My Game!

WE HAVE AN INDISPENSABLE kitchen angel, a true *paisano* named Signor Garbo. We say *indispensable* because, quite frankly, we couldn't get along without him ... or the valuable service he provides. Garbo doesn't say much, but he can handle whatever we throw at him. And we throw a lot at him: slimy egg shells, bruised and quickly browning fruit peelings, and paper towels soggy from mopping up various liquids we've spilled—to list just a few of the icky things we dump on Garbo. But our old friend takes it all in stride. He knows we need a way of getting rid of "stuff"—which is how he came into our lives in the first place.

Garbo is our kitchen trash can. He knew we had a "problem" in the form of unpleasant things that needed to be removed from our lives in the kitchen. *"I'm in da disposal bizness,"* he told us one day. *"Yeah, I know. It's a doity job, but somebody's gotta do it!"*

True, every kitchen needs a trash can, a place to put all the unpleasant things generated during the process of cooking and eating, like the stinky fish head we recently lopped off so we could finish preparing dinner. "Don't worry 'bout it," Garbo reassured us. "I'll take care of dis."

Garbo is a loner. Not that he has to be, he's an accepted and valued part of our kitchen. But he realizes that he daily has a lot of contact with some pretty vile things. He once told us, "Da stuff I'm holdin' inside me don't exactly bring out da best conversation." So he absents himself from the company of our family of kitchen angels. Signor Garbo chooses instead to hang out under the kitchen sink, behind closed cabinet doors. But when things don't go as planned, like the other day when we fumbled what should have been a routine job—making a jelly sandwich, and yes, the bread always *does* land jelly-side down—we call on Garbo to help us clean up the scene of the crime. "My job is ta help get rid of da garbage," Garbo proudly states. "An' I'm da best at whut I do."

Periodically, Garbo's contents get driven to the outskirts of town to be "dropped off"! Garbo says it's for the best: "Dat way, we get rid of all da evidence—no one's ever gonna know ya ate all dem cookies by ya-self!" Yes, it's true, Garbo is also the custodian to a few secrets which, should they ever come to light, might prove somewhat embarrassing. "Relax, will ya?" he reassures us. "I know da best way ta handle a nasty bit a bizness! After all, I'm a professional!"

Aha, Signor Garbo is a professional! And we amateurs can learn a valuable lesson from him. *We* certainly did. We once rented a movie for our Friday Date Night. It was a seemingly innocuous bit of escapist fare, but ten minutes into the story there was a totally disgusting act of violence which, although off-camera, was extremely nauseating to think about. Along with that, an overuse of vulgarity and a truly dark depiction of life had us feeling positively ill. In fact, we felt (to quote Garbo) "*absotively* doity!"

Needless to say, we immediately stopped watching the movie. Still, we almost felt like we needed a bath. Now, mind you, we're not a couple of fuddy-duddies, but there's a limit to what we're willing to toss into our heads. For one thing, it's counterproductive: just as "we are what we eat," we're also what we put into our minds; or, we are what we think about! (Proverbs 23:7)

Regardless, Garbo read us the riot act. "Whut were ya thinkin'? I collect da garbage in dis house! You ain't designed ta hold such trash." And he's right. The Word of God teaches that once we invite Jesus Christ into our hearts and lives, our Lord takes full occupancy; every follower of Christ then becomes a "temple of the Holy Spirit." (1 Corinthians 6:19) And, need we state it? God does not want to live in a trash can. "But dat's da point, you're NOT a trash can!" Garbo fumes. "Dat's my job! So stop fillin' your heads wit garbage."

Okay, okay! We get it! We should only put wholesome things into our minds. We need to stick to the Apostle Paul's formula:

Fix your thoughts on what is true, and honorable, and right, and pure, and lovely, and admirable. Think about things that are excellent and worthy of praise.
—Philippians 4:8 NLT

Garbo says, "Hey you! Yeah, *you*. You know who I'm talkin' to. You're not a trash can. So stop tryin' ta muscle in on my territory! Don't be readin' or watchin' or listenin' ta junk dat don't pass da stinkin' garbage test! Kapeesh?"

The Best Thing Since Sliced Bread

WHAT COULD BE BETTER than bread? It's called the staff of life, because throughout time, grain products have sustained people across the globe. Hop in a time machine and visit any era—in any area of the world—and you'll simply confirm that bread was (and continues to be) an important part of nearly every meal. In fact, bread was often the chief staple of those meals, sometimes complimented only by a small piece of fish or cheese. Hence, bread had value far beyond its price, eventually leading to the slang usage of the words *dough* and *bread* to signify money: "He's rolling in the dough"; or "If you want me to go shopping for you, I'll need some bread."

Biscuits, bagels, buns, and baguettes; cornbread, croutons, and crumpets; Matzah, muffins, and melba toast; tortillas, pitas, and poppadum.[2] Whether it's unleavened or yeasty, whole grain or gluten free, made from wheat, barley or rye, baked as rolls, flatbread or flakes, every nationality and every people group seems to have a favorite. Visit your local supermarket and you'll find many specialty breads: high-fiber and specialty grain products such as Ezekiel bread; artisan breads, Hawaiian rolls, and English muffins. Around Easter and Chanukah (aka Hanukkah) you'll find Challah bread. And companies such as Pepperidge Farm

---

[2] Poppadum is a very thin, flat, circular South Asian bread that easily breaks into pieces.

market seasonal breads like Pumpkin Spice and Apple Cinnamon.

We're fortunate to have all this variety. We were making sandwiches recently, and started pondering the diversity and utility of various breads. We like ham on rye, pastrami on Italian, and peanut butter on double-fiber. By the way, sandwiches were invented by a chef looking for a way to serve meats and cheeses to his employer, who insisted on eating with his fingers while playing cards—but who didn't want the playing cards to get greasy. The chef soon hit upon the idea that he could serve the Earl of Sandwich a layer of cold meat wrapped within two pieces of bread. People have been eating cards and playing sandwiches ever since—or something like that.

We use a thick-sliced Dutch Country potato bread when we're making French toast, because it's slightly denser and comes in thicker slices than regular bread. Hence it soaks up more of the egg and cinnamon mixture. And there's nothing like a slice of Wonder Bread® lightly toasted with butter and jam. Wonder Bread is plain old ultra-refined white bread. We're not sure this after-school favorite of kids still enjoys the same popularity it did 50 years ago. Sometime around the 1980s, refined bread fell out of fashion. Health-conscious people started buying whole wheat, which was more expensive at the supermarket. People who couldn't afford whole wheat were stuck with the cheap white bread which, considering the history of commercial baking, is indeed ironic.

Prior to the late 20th century, bleached and ultra-refined white bread was more expensive than its unrefined sibling, wheat bread. As a matter of fact, only "poor" people ate wheat bread. To quote a line from Mark Twain's *The Adventures of Huckleberry Finn,* white bread or "'baker's bread'—[is] what the quality eat; none of your low-down corn-pone." Thanks to Wonder Bread and other companies, however, by 1950 practically everybody was serving sliced white bread at meals. Which brings us back to our opening

15

question: What could be better than bread?

Answer: sliced bread. Don't snicker, because we've all learned it's the gold standard against which everything else is measured. When we think something is truly innovative, we proclaim, "It's the best thing since sliced bread." And just imagine, what if before you could make yourself a sandwich you had to first slice the bread. TV commercials would need to be longer to give us more time in the kitchen. Plus, you'd need one of those special bread knives or the loaf just squishes.

Thank goodness, someone had the brilliant idea of cutting out the extra work. In 1930, Wonder Bread was the first nationally-marketed bread that came pre-sliced. No wonder Wonder took off in popularity.

So many types of breads from which to choose, and yet there's another. A bread far more essential, far more beneficial, and far, far the greatest thing since sliced bread. It's the spiritual Bread of Life, represented by Jesus Christ and the Word of God. Jesus said, "People do not live by bread alone, but by every Word that comes from the mouth of God." (Matthew 4:4 NLT)

We may need baked bread to sustain our physical bodies. But we're also spiritual beings created in God's own image. Hence, we also need spiritual bread: Jesus said, "I am the Bread of Life! ...Anyone who eats the bread will live forever...." (John 6:48-51 NLT) And just as we find baked breads everywhere in life, there's nowhere we can go where God is not present. "...Neither height nor depth, nor anything else in all creation, [can] separate us from the love of God that is in Christ Jesus our Lord." (Romans 8:39 NIV)

Have you partaken of God's Bread of Life? If not, don't continue to avoid Him. Join Him at His spiritual table. And once you've received Him, remember to consume some of His spiritual *wonder bread* each day, the Word of God— it's the best thing since sliced bread!

Toast!

FEELING A BIT ON the crummy side today? Perhaps you've even begun to feel that life itself is rather crummy. You know, crummy weather, crummy traffic, crummy friends and coworkers?

We're reminded of a valuable lesson we once learned ... from Toastie, our toaster. Yes, just about everything we encounter in the kitchen (foods, cooking, and appliances) seems to help illustrate truths about life, love, and relationships. And our faithful little toaster is no different. We use the word *faithful*, because if we were to call him our "Brave Little Toaster," Walt Disney Studios could sue us. And we'd be miserable begging on a street corner. No, really.

Besides, "faithful" truly fits our toaster. He's waiting for us, there in the kitchen, each morning. Always ready to serve us our daily bread at the flip of a lever—golden brown, never burnt. Always cheerful with a positive attitude—at least, that's how we choose to imagine him.

Most of the time. Some mornings, however, it's as though our toaster woke up on the wrong side of the counter. He has this stinking attitude, as though something's smoldering inside. Oh yeah, and on such mornings, he apparently takes his bad day out on us, by burning our toast! We dare not say anything, though, because he might start flinging sliced bread in our faces.

What's his problem? Clearly our toaster is feeling a bit crummy. Let's define "crummy": miserable or wretched; shabby, inferior, or ... even worthless.

Hey, lil' guy, you're not inferior—you're wonderful! So, what's got you down?

He's not talking. So we'll need to use a little toaster psychology. That's when we remember that another, older definition of *crummy* is "full of crumbs"! Yes, *that's it!*

Now, whenever our toaster starts to smoke and emit the smell of burnt bread, we remove the tray from his base and, sure enough, it's filled with crumbs.

In order to keep Toastie, our *dear, devoted* and *dedicated* toaster,[3] happy and performing at the top of his game, we have to periodically shake off the crumbs that accumulate around his metallic feet—er, base. We follow this step with a gentle wipe-down of his tray, and then return him to the appliance garage located atop the kitchen counter. *Wait a second.* Please excuse us. "The Masked Toaster" insists we call it the Avengers Tower—headquarters of that famed team of culinary crime fighters, the Mighty Thor (our blender), Captain Can-Opener, and the invincible Iron Griddle! (No, we are *not* looney. But our appliances *are* a bit eccentric.)

Getting back to what we asked you at the beginning of this article, "Feeling a bit on the crummy side today?" If so, understand that it's not just toasters that can accumulate crumbs. In life, we too need to periodically shake off the crumbs of hurts, disappointments, and offenses; which can pile up and keep us from performing at the top of our

---

[3] What can we say? Toastie proofread this book and made a few choice edits of his own.

game. We won't "function" properly, or accomplish any-thing, all because we're too busy fuming over the things in life that didn't work out, or just don't seem fair, or right.

If you allow the, sometimes, crummy circumstances, consequences, and comedowns of life to pile up in your heart, these things will begin to smolder inside you. Soon you'll be "burning up" emotionally; "smoking" over past mis-takes, hurts, and disappointments. And, like our toaster, you'll start stinking in your thinking. Follow that darkened path *and you'll end up as toast!*

Things don't always work out as we planned. And we don't always get what we want. But, to quote a pseudo-Chinese proverb, "That's the way the cookie crumbles"—leaving behind ... *crumbs*. Furthermore, at one time or another, we encounter "crumbs" in the form of people who are uncaring, insensitive, and downright rude. In fact, the word *crumb* can be defined as an untrustworthy or con-temptible person. And—even when interacting with good friends and family—we can slowly accumulate the crumbs of offenses, which can lead to unforgiveness and eventually to bitterness; which can burn us up emotionally. When this happens, we're toast!

The disciples of Christ faced this problem, as they trav-eled from place to place spreading the Gospel. Some towns accepted them and extended hospitality. Others rudely re-jected the disciples and their message. We can imagine this rejection was both bewildering and upsetting. Perhaps it even angered these men. Who could blame them? Have you ever tried to bless someone with an act of kindness, and received nothing in return but ingratitude and scorn? Well, again, sometimes that's the way the cookie crumbles.

Jesus understood how quickly and easily the crumbs of offenses can pile up; and He didn't want His disciples "smoking" over these social slights. So He admonished His followers, "If people do not welcome you, leave ... and shake the dust off your feet...." (Luke 9:5 NIV) Jesus used the analogy of "dust" to represent rejection, disappointments, and the ill feelings left whenever we encounter a general lack of hospitality.

He could have just as well said, "Shake off the crumbs!" Of course, at the time, no one would have understood what in the world He meant—because no one owned a toaster 2,000 years ago.

Regardless, God doesn't want you burning up inside, fuming over people who've wronged you, and stinking in your thinking. That means you can't allow the crumbs to get inside your spirit. So, when hurts come, or things just don't go as you planned or hoped for, shake the crumbs off your feet and keep moving forward. "Pursue peace with all, ...lest any root of bitterness springing up should trouble you...." (Hebrews 12:14-15 BLB)

A Stirring Message

RECENTLY WE SHARED a mug of coffee made by our pal Comrade Keurig. You remember our friend Keurig? When we first introduced this kitchen angel, in "The Call of the Keurig,"[4] he was "finding his voice." On this particular day, he was making us our favorite Hazelnut Breakfast Blend.

The beauty of our Keurig is that we can add the creamer and our favorite sweetener to the mug, place the mug before him, and then he does all the rest: he adds the perfect amount of water, at the perfect brewing temperature, and he does it all in a quick minute with no cleanup required.

---

[4] Featured in *Angel in the Kitchen*.

This time around, however, something wasn't quite right. We each took a sip and frowned. Our breakfast brew was bitter!

We distinctly remembered adding stevia to the mug before handing it over to our Keurig, so we were a little confused. "Hey, Comrade Keurig!" we cried. "What happened?"

Our Keurig didn't answer. He just sat there, mutely staring at us from his place on the counter.

After several awkward moments of silence, one of us asked, "What did we say? Did we somehow upset him?"

Then Comrade Keurig let out a sigh of exasperation. Actually, it was more of a loud *shoooosh!*

"What's he trying to tell us?" we wondered.

Translating native Keurig is more of an art than a science, and in order to grasp the full meaning of each little utterance, one must also take into consideration the circumstances in which the words are spoken. "Dear Keurig, can you please give us another hint?" we pleaded gently.

It was at this point that we noticed the spoon resting on the counter next to our friend. Clearly, Keurig was also making note of it—as well as the fact that it was dry. "Didn't you *stir* the mug?" we asked.

Turns out none of us had stirred our breakfast blend. And upon realizing this, it wasn't hard to catch the full meaning of Keurig's cry.

"Come on," he said. "Can you please give me a break here? I daily bless you with the perfect cup of coffee. But you guys need to do your part, too. You gotta stir the stuff up! Okay?"

"Our dear Comrade Keurig," we exclaimed. "You have so much wisdom to share!"

How could we have forgotten such an important step in all things culinary? Face it, you can't have *stir* fry unless you stir the veggies, which otherwise would simply be lounging in the sauna—er, wok! And how about all those mixes in the cupboard? Clearly stated on the back of each box is the not-so-cryptic word stir Some of these packages go even further: the instructions on the boxes of both the instant oatmeal and the hot cocoa mix admonish us to "stir and enjoy!" (The exclamation mark is even supplied by the manufacturer.)

Our "manufacturer" (that would be God, the Creator of the Universe) gives each of us exactly the same advice. "Therefore, I remind you to you stir up the gift of God which is in you.... For God has not given us the spirit of fear; but of power, and of love, and of a sound mind." (2 Timothy 1:6 NKJV)

God has given us the perfect ingredients for an abundant life (John 10:10). He's given each of us unique gifts, talents, abilities, and callings. But we must do our part if we are to enjoy what God has provided: we need to stir up the treasure poured into each of us. And we stir things up spiritually by *using* our gifts, *answering* our callings, and in general, *exercising* our faith. When we don't, things have a way of "settling to the bottom" of our lives. As the old expression goes, "Use it or lose it."

Don't be shy about using your talents and pursuing the things God has called you to do. Don't be afraid of failure —we can learn and benefit from our own mistakes. And never fear the opinions of others. Instead, expand your horizons, stretch your spiritual wings, and follow your dreams. Be the person God designed you to be.

And don't forget to stir your relationships—in order to properly blend together: "And we should think toward stirring up one another to love and to good works, not forsaking the assembling together of ourselves as is the custom with some, but encouraging one another...." (Hebrews 10:24-25 BLB) In other words, hang out with other believers, people who can encourage you; and be sure to encourage them. Become a cheerleader for those who are pursuing a dream or simply trying to achieve something meaningful in life.

Especially encourage the people on "God's team," the believers who often struggle to live a God-centered life in order to make a difference in the lives of others through their giving and serving. Together we can bring out the best in each other.

Stir up your faith by listening to encouraging messages such as those presented on television by CBN, TBN and other inspirational networks. Have a personal time of devotion with God—and share these times with your family. And don't forsake the assembling of God's spiritual family. (Hebrews 10:25) Attend a Bible-based faith community with a loving congregation; and take part in the programs and activities there. When believers live, worship, pray, and work together, they can stir their communities to become peaceful and productive places in which to live.

Please do your part. Stir up your faith, love, and special gifts. When you do, you'll create quite a stir in the world. You'll also have the thanks and admiration of our kitchen angel, Comrade Keurig.

Of Rice and Relationships

WE CAUSED QUITE A STIR with "A Stirring Message," in which we discussed the importance of stirring things up: certain foods and beverages require stirring to obtain the proper flavor and consistency; similarly, each of us should "stir up" the gifts and talents God has bestowed, in order to bring out our best and most consistent qualities.

However, when it comes to other methods of cooking, we get the best results by *not* stirring. For example, good cooks agree that if you want to prepare rice that's fluffy, not gooey and sticky, the secret to success is simple: *don't stir the pot!*

Rice is a staple food in numerous countries, including the Dominican Republic and Puerto Rico, respectively the birthplaces of Wilma's father and mother. In their cultures, serving sticky rice is an unpardonable sin, which is why Wilma's *Mamita* taught her the secret to good rice: fill the pot with just enough water to cover the rice, bring the water to a boil, add the rice, gently mix it, reduce the heat, cover it—*and then leave it alone!* Do. Not. Stir. It!

Stirring the rice mixture will upset the proper balance of steam, and also cause the release of excess starch, which results in the grains becoming gooey and sticking together. But for many cooks, following this simple tip is easier said than done. Some of us just can't resist removing the lid and stirring things up. And the same can be said in regards to our relationships with friends, family, and coworkers.

The secret to success in all social interactions is simple: don't stir the pot. Ignoring this basic truth can lead to some sticky situations and generally makes a gooey mess of things.

The well-known idiom "stirring the pot" can be defined as: promoting feelings of annoyance, agitation or dissatisfaction; by encouraging tension and conflict between two or more people—or groups of people—in order to make trouble or to elicit a strong emotional reaction. Simply put, "stirring the pot" involves any words or actions intended to get someone emotionally worked up.

We all know someone in life, next door, at the job, down the street, who seems to take great pleasure in stirring things up. They revel in creating strife, division, and needless drama. Sometimes these people are just bored, so they try to liven things up at someone else's expense. Sometimes the "pot stirrer" has more selfish reasons, and hopes to gain some advantage over another person. Sometimes, however, there are more devious psychological motivations at work. For instance, because "misery loves company," a discontented person will do his best to stir up discontent.

Pot stirring can take many forms, such as teasing or "joking" about an emotionally painful relationship or situation; making provocative statements intended to fuel the flames of discord; or ... repeating gossip.

Spreading rumors—or simply repeating the news about someone's problems, setbacks, and relational confrontations—can stir up more bitterness, more strife and more division. It also hinders God's ability to heal emotional wounds and bring unity.

The Bible gives a strong warning to would-be pot stirrers: "There are six things the Lord <u>hates</u>—no, seven: haughtiness, lying, murdering, plotting evil, eagerness to do wrong, a false witness, <u>sowing discord among brothers</u>." (Proverbs 6:16-19 TLB) This, of course, is not an all-inclusive list of the actions and attitudes that grieve our Lord. But interestingly, stated together in this single verse, are several offenses which clearly define the act of stirring the pot. And if God "hates" these things, we can assume that He does not prosper the pot stirrer. In fact, the opposite is true: God bestows His particular blessings on the peacemaker.

"Blessed (enjoying enviable happiness, spiritually prosperous—with life-joy and satisfaction in God's favor and salvation, regardless of their outward conditions) are the makers and maintainers of peace, for they shall be called the sons of God!" (Matthew 5:9 AMPC) Let's receive this as the primary lesson of God's "Pot Principles."

The second lesson is for all those of us who at one time or another have been on the receiving end of pot stirring. If you've been the victim of gossip, or falsely accused, or punished for doing the right thing, God wants you to keep your cool and remain in peace; to paraphrase the fictional secret agent James Bond, shaken—*but not stirred*. Life is not always fair, but then, you knew that. Right? Furthermore, God is our advocate; He is always just, so we need to trust Him to vindicate us in any given situation. The Biblical Joseph did this, and things worked out better than he could have imagined. You can read his hair-raising life story in Genesis 37-50.

The third lesson of God's Pot Principles dovetails nicely with #2. It's always best to let God do the stirring. Be stirred by His Word, by His goodness, power, and wisdom. "He is the Rock; His deeds are perfect. Everything He does is just and fair. He is a faithful God who does no wrong; how just and upright He is!" (Deuteronomy 32:4 NLT)

And remember, stirring the pot is bad for both rice and relationships.

Stir up Yourself, and awake to my vindication, to my cause, my God and my Lord. Vindicate me, O LORD my God, according to Your righteousness; And let them not rejoice over me.
—Psalm 35:23-24 NKJV

Foiled!

"An Ode to Aluminum Foil"[5]

Come and listen to a story about a man named Jed,
An overworked cook who daily packed his fam'ly's bread.
Then one day he was wrapping up some food,
So off from the roll he tore somethin' good!
—Foil, that is ... alum'num ... Reynolds Wrap.®

RELAX, DEAR READER. We have no intentions of pursuing songwriting. But we would like to share a few words about aluminum foil, the unsung hero of cooks everywhere.

Aluminum foil is one of the most versatile materials we know. And it has several uses in both the kitchen and the commercial packaging of foods. It insulates and protects, preventing certain foods from burning due to uneven heating. It keeps foods fresher for longer periods, because it blocks the rays necessary for the growth of bacteria. And yet it's extremely thin and lightweight. In fact, "heavy-duty" aluminum foil is less than one thousandth of an inch thick.

Aluminum foil was first manufactured in Switzerland, in 1910, as thin yet strong metal leaves. Because of its thinness, aluminum foil folds and shapes easily, allowing cooks to tightly wrap everything from a turkey drumstick to a hoagie sandwich. The Swiss candy manufacturer, Tobler,

---

[5] Sung to the tune of "The Ballad of Jed Clampett" from the 1960s TV sitcom *The Beverly Hillbillies.*

was the first company to use the material in commercial food packaging; in 1911, Tobler started wrapping its unique, triangular-shaped Toblerone® chocolates in aluminum foil.

Prior to the advent of aluminum foil, foods were frequently packaged in tinfoil. But prior to and during World War II, tin was infamous for imparting a metallic taste to the foods it was in contact with. So, by 1950, aluminum foil was rapidly replacing its dull sibling in both homes and commercial food packaging. Here in the U.S., we sometimes erroneously refer to any and all aluminum foil as Reynolds Wrap®, but that's actually the registered brand name of the Reynolds Metal company, which has always been the chief manufacturer and supplier of kitchen foil in the U.S. Interestingly, in the UK it's often still called "tin" foil, for the same reason people still refer to tin cans—even though all cans used in food storage today are either made of steel or aluminum. (Old habits die hard, right?)

Dear aluminum. How we do malign your shiny metal.

We use aluminum foil to wrap our sandwiches, but before anyone begins to wonder why we don't use plastic sandwich baggies, please let us explain. Those saggy sandwich baggies are ... *baggy!* They don't hold the sandwich firmly and securely. The bread, meats, and cheese sit loosely in the bag, with nothing to really keep the components together. Stick a poor sandwich into a baggie and toss it into your lunch bag, basket or backpack and here's what happens: during the course of your travels, as you hike, bike, or drive over winding roads or bumpy trails, your sandwich flops about in its saggy baggie until it falls apart. Not so if you securely wrap it in foil!

A sandwich firmly wrapped in aluminum foil holds together! The meat, cheese, lettuce, tomato, pickle, and onion stay put—instead of falling apart. When you remove it from its foil, your sandwich *looks* like a sandwich—not a loosely shuffled deck of playing cards. And the bread doesn't get mangled and all bent out of shape!

We may seem overly enthused about the merits of aluminum foil, but there's something we're far more passionate about: our Heavenly Father! *God is the believer's "reynolds wrap."* He protects and preserves us! "You are a hiding place for me; you preserve me from trouble; you surround me with shouts of deliverance." (Psalm 32:7 ESV)

Like aluminum foil, God holds us securely in His arms and keeps us from falling apart as we travel the bumpy road of life. "...God is your refuge, and His everlasting arms are under you." (Deuteronomy 33:27 NLT) There's no lack of stress and adversity in this hectic world, and it's easy to get "wrapped up" in the cares of life; but when we put our trust in Jesus Christ and focus on God instead of on our circumstances and problems, He's capable of holding us together and keeping us from getting all bent out of shape. "These things I have spoken unto you, that in Me you might have peace. In the world you shall have tribulation: but be of good cheer; I have overcome the world." (John 16:33 KJ2000)

God also *insulates* us from the power of sin! His redeeming blood covers us and keeps us from burning. "...We have redemption through His blood, the forgiveness of sins." (Ephesians 1:7 KJ) "[God's] love covers all offenses." (Proverbs 10:12 ESV)

Feel like a sandwich today? We do, secure in the knowledge that God (our divine "reynolds wrap") is more than able to foil all the schemes of the enemy!

We have this hope as an anchor for the soul, <u>firm and secure</u>....
—Hebrews 6:19 NIV)

Truly He is my rock and my salvation; He is my fortress, <u>I will not be shaken</u>.
—Psalm 62:6 NIV

Reports of Strange Kitchen Phenomena

SCIENTIST AND SCIENCE FICTION novelist Arthur C. Clarke once wrote, "Any sufficiently advanced technology is indistinguishable from magic." The author used this astute observation as a plot device in many of his stories and novels, including *2001: A Space Odyssey* (both the book and the movie). But what exactly constitutes "sufficiently advanced" tech? We imagine it's practically anything beyond human knowledge.

But we all have different life experiences; and as a result, what *we* know may not be what *you* know. For instance, there are things going on in our kitchen that we can't quite understand. Seemingly magical changes are taking place before our very eyes; processes as ancient as time itself, and yet beyond our limited knowledge.

Join us now, as we journey into the deepest recesses of the kitchen, and plumb the depths of the curious and arcane. Keep a firm grip on both your flashlight and your sanity, for we shall encounter the unexplainable, the unimaginable, perhaps even ... the unspeakable.

Actually, we're more likely to encounter the unspeakable in the laundry room, when we take a load of clothes from the dryer. Yes, by the Rings of Saturn, crouching atop the pile of sheets and towels are ... (Oh, the horror. Dare we say it?) some of our *unmentionables.*

Ahem, on to the kitchen, brave heart.

There ... in the cabinet ... can you see it?!? Dear Lord, it's a box of ... gelatine. And next to it—*Gasp!*—baking powder. What manner of witchcraft be lurking in yon cupboard?

Have you ever noticed the strange sorcery that takes place when boiling water is added to gelatin? Out of sight within the dark regions of the refrigerator, the steaming liquid cools, and slowly transforms into a semi-solid jiggling mass of allegedly edible dessert ... with a fruity flavor that is not its own. Okay, we do know it's not magic, but rather science. We also realize we can google the chemistry behind gelatin, but.... Seriously, we don't really care, because we already know what we need to know: Jell-O® works every time. Like magic. We're not sure how, but we have confidence that mixing this little powder with some H_2O produces gelatine. *Onward.*

Dost thou understand what gibbering madness cries out for baking powder to be added to the cauldron in which thou mixeth a batch of brownies? What dost the baking powder actually do? For that matter, precisely what is baking powder? We actually know this one. Yet, many cooks don't. They simply follow the age-old wisdom of the cookbook. They may not understand all the *hows, whys* and *wherefores,* but these people have been promised good results by a chef much wiser than them, and they have faith that any given recipe will work.

Call it kitchen faith.

The reason things work in the kitchen is because they are backed by natural laws. We trust in these natural laws —even though we may not understand all the principles behind them. And we know it's not magic, but rather an as-yet-unlearned part of the puzzle revealing life's great mysteries. Interestingly, not too many seem bothered by not knowing the reasons behind all the intricate workings within the average kitchen. They're too busy enjoying all the tasty benefits of the kitchen.

Regarding the spiritual realm, most of us have far more questions than answers. There are Biblical principles, the reasons for which we may not know or fully understand. Furthermore, God has promised things that seem impossible. He can take our mistakes and use our circumstances to make our lives nicely "gel" into something wonderful. How does He do it? Why does He do it? Do we really need to know in order to enjoy His blessings? "Trust in the LORD with all your heart; do not depend on your own understanding." (Proverbs 3:5 NLT)

Most of the answers are in His Holy Word, but there will always be a little mystery to His divine workings. Some things we just won't know for sure until we go home to spend eternity with our Heavenly Father. But, like all the cooks who have kitchen faith, we should have faith in God's promises and precepts. We may not be able to see and understand the intricacies behind them, but we should realize they are not "magic"; but rather truths backed by God's divine laws and supernatural principles.

You don't need to know or understand every single truth in the Bible in order to start enjoying the blessings of a life spent with God. For instance, you can accept salvation without knowing when Christ will return, and if it will be *before* or *after* what theologians call The Great Tribulation. You can have faith in God's promises without knowing all the hows, whys, and wherefores. Simply follow the age-old wisdom of the spiritual cookbook (the Word of God). Trust what it says, and you'll have good results—because the "Master Chef," who is much wiser than any of us, has promised that all His "recipes" will work.

"'My thoughts are nothing like your thoughts,' says the LORD. 'And my ways are far beyond anything you could imagine.'" (Isaiah 55:8 NLT)

A Panini for the People

EVER SINCE WE LAUNCHED our book and internet series Angel in the Kitchen by announcing that our toaster can talk, another member of our eccentric ensemble of kitchen angels has been asking for equal time. He states quite humbly that while Lil' Toastee can brown a bagel, crisp a crumpet, or make ... well, toast, *he* can perfectly prepare a gourmet sandwich. All his boasting aside, however, Signor Panini *is* pretty awesome, and he wants a chance to share his message with the world. It's a bit of wisdom well worth relating, too. So, here now with his very own story, is that master of the glamorous grill set, Signor Panini! [Meanwhile, we the "editors" will be standing by should we be needed.]

Buongiorno! I am a panini-maker! That's a fancy title for a two-sided warming grill that heats—what else?—scrumptious panini sandwiches. Maybe that doesn't sound like a big deal, but the panini is well known in most English-speaking countries, and anyone who's ever had one knows they are simply the best. Far better than some peanut butter spread across a piece of dry toast that's gonna stick to the roof of your mouth—no matter what that antiquated chrome-faced toaster—-

[Okay, stop right there, Signor Panini. *Basta!* Enough! No mud-slinging or name-calling allowed. Please stick to the issues or we'll be forced to place you back in the cabinet.]

Sigh, I should have listened to my mother. She wanted me to be a pasta-roller. Anyway, a panini is a grilled sandwich made from bread other than sliced bread. Yeah, you can use plain bread like that high-and-mighty Lil'—-

[Ahem!]

Well, a great panini begins with specialty breads such as baguette, ciabatta, or michetta. The bread is split horizontally and filled with succulent meats, cheeses, and veggies such as olives and sautéed mushrooms. My editors prefer my London Broil panini: mouthwatering beef layered on thick-sliced olive bread, topped with onions and red peppers.

They also like my Cubano. That's a Cuban sandwich made with ham, sliced or pulled pork, Swiss cheese, garlic pickles, and a blend of mayo and Dijon mustard—on French bread. (Hey, diversity, right?) A Cubano is basically a panini with a Spanish accent.

But without me, none of these wonderful ingredients would ever reach their full potential. A sandwich is a sandwich, but a sandwich prepared by me is a gourmet treat. The secret to my ability to transform the ordinary into the extraordinary lies in my design: I have two—count 'em—two grilling surfaces. These square heating surfaces, called *platens*, are hinged at one side. I have a platen below—upon which the sandwich is placed—and a platen above. When my upper platen is lowered, the sandwich is completely surrounded—like a gangster in an FBI movie.

Then I go to work. I apply heat and pressure from every side. My heated platens, above and below, ensure the sandwich ingredients evenly and properly cook. And the press of the weighted platens helps the bread to turn crispy and golden-brown without burning. Of course, I'm only as good as the people using me. Fortunately, my editors are usually hovering nearby, and know when to open me and remove their delicious panini sandwich. I'm pretty foolproof that way, which is important when dealing with my editors.

[Allowing Signor Panini to have his say may have been a bad idea.]

Heat and pressure from every side is the secret to my success. And guess what, life is a lot like a panini maker. People encounter obstacles every single day and in every single pursuit. They face trials in their health, finances, jobs, relationships.... You name it. Things can get pretty hot, and it often seems as though every which way you turn, you encounter the pressures of life.

Ever feel like you're being squeezed a little? Like you're caught between a rock and a hard place? Like a panini in a New York delicatessen? It happens in life, but you can take comfort in the words of the Apostle Paul. He faced opposition from both the Gentiles and many of the Jewish religious leaders; and challenges in both the secular world and the earliest gatherings of believers. Like a spiritual panini, Paul was pressured on both sides. He confessed, "We are pressed on every side by troubles, but we are not crushed. We are perplexed, but not driven to despair. We are hunted down, but never abandoned by God. We get knocked down, but we are not destroyed." (2 Corinthians 4:8-9 NLT)

In spite of feeling like a human panini, Paul didn't get *bitter*—he got *better*. Regarding his innumerable trials, he states, "Despite all these things, overwhelming victory is ours through Christ, who loved us." (Romans 8:37) Paul overcame every challenge while keeping a victorious attitude because he realized his loving Heavenly Father always had His hand on "life's panini maker." No matter how hot things seemed to get, no matter how much pressure was being applied, Paul understood he was "never abandoned by God." (2 Corinthians 4:9) Paul's Creator was in the process of transforming the ordinary ingredients of the apostle's life into something extraordinary. Furthermore, God is the Master Chef—and He knows just when to lift the top platen and remove His "gourmet" masterpieces.

Paul writes, "No test or temptation [or trial] that comes your way is beyond the course of what others have had to face. All you need to remember is that God will never let you down; He will never let you be pushed past your limit; He will always be there to help you come through it." (1 Corinthians 10:13 MSG) In other words, God never lets a "panini" get burnt.

If you're going through a season of being "pressed on every side by troubles," and you can feel the heat of your problems surrounding you, take heart: "For it is God who is working in you, enabling you both to desire and to work out His good purpose." (Philippians 2:13 HCSB)

[*Grazie* for this encouraging truth, Signor Panini.]

Mmmpph! Excuse me. Can't talk now— my mouth is full of food!

Dear reader, all trials eventually pass, and God is always with you in the midst of adversity. Furthermore, "We know that in all things God works for the good of those who love him...." (Romans 8:28 NIV) So cling to God's Word and His promises. And keep the faith!

Served on the Everyday Dishes

WE LOVE PRETTY CHINA, and over the years we've collected several sets of dinnerware with beautiful patterns ranging from song birds and roses to winter fowl and fishes. And we actually use them throughout the year. We put out different patterns for different seasons, holidays and occasions. We're not being snooty, we just enjoy setting a pretty table. Plus, we know that setting out nice plates makes our guests feel very special.

However, we're not averse to using paper plates. In fact, for certain situations paper plates (or plates molded from plastic or Styrofoam) are best. And face it, most people who own fine china usually also have a set of everyday dishes—nothing to really brag about, but perfectly serviceable for setting a meal on the table.

Now, allow us to ask you two important questions. Your answers will be key to the kitchen wisdom we're about to share. 1) What's more important, the food or what it's served on? 2) Does serving food on a paper or foam plate make it taste any less delicious?

If you're like us, you'd rather have something really scrumptious served on everyday dishes than something that tastes ho-hum served on expensive China. We believe anybody would. Furthermore, we have friends who are good cooks but who don't own fancy dinnerware. They serve delectable meals on old plates that are scuffed, chipped and cracked—or they simply use disposable plates. Now obviously, the delicious food they lovingly prepared for us, tastes every bit as good on a chipped plate as it would if it were served to us on bone China.

So, again, while having fine China or pretty dinnerware is nice, it's not as important as the food itself—or the one who lovingly served it. If you receive something that's gourmet, it's remains gourmet whether it's served on a plate made of paper, foam, plastic, or porcelain; whether it's served in an aluminum pie pan, a chipped dish, or a bowl made of unglazed clay. The *food* served in the vessel remains unchanged.

Our Heavenly Father understands this—even when we sometimes don't. 2,000 years ago, God served the human race something that was *gourmet all the way:* the redeeming work of His only son Jesus Christ, who died for our sins that we might have eternal life. We receive God's gourmet salvation, as a free gift, when we confess with our mouths Jesus as Lord and believe in our hearts that God raised Him from the dead. (Romans 10:9) Our promise of eternal life is sealed by the power and the presence of God's Holy Spirit, who dwells within each of us.

Just think, if you're a believer, the divine Creator of the Universe is dwelling in you. God filled you with His holy presence the moment you received Christ as Lord and Savior. And it's gourmet all the way. We essentially become God's dinnerware. We doubt any of us can brag about being expensive bone China, though. Most of us are just plain, everyday dishes. Many of us are scratched and scuffed up from years of use. Some of us are cracked and a little tarnished from the often rough-handling we receive in life, or chipped and broken from our own past hurts and failings. But that's not a problem for God. He still uses each of us to serve in His kingdom.

We are God's imperfect vessels, and like plates made of paper, foam, plastic or bone China, all of us are different. "A large house contains not only vessels of gold and silver, but also of wood and clay." (2 Timothy 2:20 BSB) But does that make what we hold—the essence of the Living God, lovingly served to us by our Heavenly Father—any less wonderful? No way. "We now have this light shining in our hearts, but we ourselves are like fragile clay jars containing this great treasure." (2 Corinthians 4:7 NLT)

Easy Off!

ONCE UPON A TIME, in a kitchen far, far away ... we had one of those old-style ovens that had to be manually cleaned. We'd spray this cleaning product onto the walls of the oven —the label stated "no scrubbing necessary"—then close the door and switch on the heat. An hour or two later there was this nasty-looking sludge caked to the oven walls, which had to be sponged off. It was dark-brown and slimy and downright disgusting. We'd wear gloves while wiping the oven clean, but always managed to get greasy glop on our exposed arms.

But hey, it had to be done. A clean oven is a happy oven. Not to mention that a clean oven functions more efficiently —and doesn't embarrass you when guests peak inside it to see what's for dinner. So we really didn't mind doing it. Well, maybe just a little. All right, all right, we *hated* it.

Then one day Sparky came into our lives. No, he's not a professional oven cleaner—he *IS* our oven. And he's self-cleaning! Which is a real blessing because, face it, in life stuff happens. For instance, while baking an apple pie, the lava-hot filling often bursts through the crust, flowing through the rack like magma to the oven floor below, where it hardens into rock.

Not a problem. Sparky goes into his self-cleaning mode at the flip of a switch. When he does, he goes into full lockdown. You couldn't pry his door open with a crowbar. And that's when things *really* get hot—literally. We usually give Sparky plenty of space while he's self-cleaning, about a four-hour process in which our oven incinerates all the crud that's built up inside of him during the course of his kitchen duties.

Know what? That's right, people are like ovens: in life, we tend to build up a crusty layer of stuff, and we need cleaning if we're to be happy (like Sparky) and function efficiently. Things in life have a way of getting messy just like that apple pie filling. Regrets and feelings of hurt, guilt and shame can bubble over and leave us feeling "cruddy"; and if not dealt with, this layer of gunk can separate us, or make us feel distant, from our Heavenly Father.

But unlike Sparky, not a single one of us has a self-cleaning feature. Oh, some of us *think* we do. We have a relative who once mentioned that he plans to get "right" with God one day, and even start going to church, but *first* he needs to "clean up his act." Don't we all? But that is *not* a prerequisite for being accepted by God. Our Heavenly Father is waiting for us with open arms. He's inviting us to come as we are. "...He has made us accepted in the beloved." (Ephesians 1:6 AKJ)

Some of us believe we can't face God until we get out of an improper relationship, or stop drinking, abusing drugs, etc. Only we're like those old-fashioned ovens. We're good at cooking up a mess—even when we're trying to be good—but we don't have the right "formula" to de-gunk ourselves; or the "muscle" needed to scrub the innermost parts of our lives.

Not to worry. God does. And He has *never* expected us to *try* to clean up our own messes before approaching Him. That's why He sent us His only Son as a Savior. Jesus

Christ is the real, *spiritual*, "easy off"—with absolutely no scrubbing or wiping necessary. Don't allow anyone to tell you otherwise.

But again, that's why God accepts us as we are: *who* we are and *where* we are. He recognizes a good oven when He sees one, despite the grime on the inside. After the "oven" (person) is in "His house," then He sets about cleaning it ... until it sparkles like new. And as with an oven, He cleans us from the inside out. In other words, God loves us as we are, but He loves us too much to let us stay that way.

"'Come now, let's settle this,' says the Lord. 'Though your sins are like scarlet, I will make them as white as snow....'" (Isaiah 1:18 KJV)

Are you feeling gunked up today? Not functioning as smoothly as you should? Call out to your Heavenly Father. He collects ovens of all colors and models, and then restores them to show-room condition: sparkling clean inside and out.

This means that anyone who belongs to Christ has become a <u>new</u> person. The old life is gone; a new life has begun!
—2 Corinthians 5:17 NLT

Night and the Kitchen

SOME LITTLE TIME AGO the sun disappeared behind the line of trees bordering our home, and now the whole world—or so it seems—has been plunged into darkness. Night has fallen. Silent and impenetrable, like a heavy suffocating shroud.

In our kitchen, also, darkness covers the countertops and veils the cabinets. We can easily imagine the appliances all slumbering, each of them tucked away ... waiting for a new dawn.

And yet, there's a ghostly light, glowing faint and green. It manifests itself as a set of cryptic numbers, which appear to hover motionless against the night ... until a single digit changes ... advancing the time, keeping track of the long hours before the faithful sun reappears in the east.

"2:10 a.m." announces the clock above the range.

Unseen by us, Sparky (the gas range) has been keeping watch. While most of the surrounding world sleeps, he lies awake, maintaining the optimum pressure of propane in his lines, ready to flame on at a moment's notice, should one of us need him in the wee hours. Perhaps he's contemplating the fried eggs he'll help to prepare in the morning; or perhaps he simply lies quietly, sensing the presence of another appliance huddled in the darkness, biding its time till breakfast.

Sparky flashes the time, 2:11 a.m., to his patient kitchen mate, Comrade Keurig, who's been keeping the water in his reservoir nice and hot, lest he be unprepared to make us cocoa after we suddenly awaken from a bad dream. He gently whispers a prayer that sounds like the swish of an angel's wings; and Sparky smiles, knowing his friend has had too much caffeine.

From across the room a dull groan pierces the darkness, followed by a startling *ker-chunk!* 2:12 a.m.... Fridgey has been making ice all along, while preserving the foods entrusted to his care. Like Sparky and Keurig, he never sleeps. He stays on duty 24/7, patiently waiting, preparing, preserving, and protecting throughout the night.

These angels in the kitchen are always ready to spring into action at a moment's notice. They understand we need them, and never need a lot of coaxing to meet our needs.

In life, too, "night" has a way of creeping in. We suddenly find ourselves facing difficult problems, and the future starts to look bleak. The Son (of God) seems to have disappeared for a time, and we can sense a spiritual darkness falling around us "Silent and impenetrable, like a heavy suffocating shroud." We feel alone, perhaps even fearful, and we begin to doubt everything we know and believe in.

But we're never alone in the dark hours of life. God is always present—even if we can't see Him or feel His presence. And like those faithful appliances in the kitchen, He's always working on our behalf, looking out for our best interests, constantly able and ready to "supply all your needs from his glorious riches, which have been given to us in Christ Jesus." (Philippians 4:19 NLT) And, as Keurig seems to know, He's only a whispered prayer away.

Our Heavenly Father encourages each of us to "Call to Me, and I will answer you, and show you great and mighty things...." (Jeremiah 33:3 AKJV) Furthermore, He's always listening and answering—24/7—because He never sleeps. (Psalm 121:4 NLT) Instead, God quietly and patiently continues to care for us throughout our darkest hours.

So when the night closes in, call out to the Creator of the Universe. Like Fridgey, Sparky and Comrade Keurig, the Lord is always present, always vigilant, always "preparing, preserving, and protecting [us] throughout the night." Never lose faith, and never forget: "The light shines in the darkness, and the darkness can never extinguish it." (John 1:5 NLT)

A new day will soon dawn. Start it—and every day—by looking up. Look to God both day and night, remembering He's always on the job. Follow the example of the Psalmist, who wrote: "I lift up my eyes to the hills.... [Because] My help comes from the LORD. ...He who keeps you will not slumber. Behold, he who keeps Israel will neither slumber nor sleep." (Psalm 121:1-4 ESV)

Pizza, People, and a Pretty Pooch

SEVERAL YEARS AGO, we adopted a gorgeous Shetland Sheepdog from a breeder and trainer. Misty, as we renamed her, had been raised in a very different and somewhat limited environment. She was used to certain foods and routines, and she was more used to being confined long hours in a crate than to having the run of the house. Now that Misty was living with us, she needed to adjust to new things and new ways and, mainly, having more freedom. Misty needed to get used to everything being different. But her period of adjustment took over a year; for months, each new room she encountered in our home seemed to unnerve her. She tended to hang out in only one room, and typically a certain corner of that room. When we'd walk into a different room, Misty acted like she wanted to follow us, but she would refuse to enter new territory.

"Want to sit on the sofa with us, Misty? Just long enough to get a family photo?" Not really. "Want to go for a walk in the woods, Misty?" Um, lemme think about it— I've never gone down this particular trail, and it's ... well, *it's different.*

Eventually, using lots of love and patience, we coaxed Misty out of her shell, and got her used to embracing new experiences. But until then, whenever Misty encountered something she wasn't familiar with, we'd chuckle and say in unison—in a cute, playful tone, as though Misty herself were saying the words—"It's different!"

Misty, lounging on her favorite window seat: "Hey, is that pizza I smell?"

We've met people who have the same outlook on life as our pooch. We know someone who loves Tex-Mex cuisine, and has dined at some pretty authentic Mexican restaurants. This person *knows* what a good *chile relleno* tastes like ... with refried beans and fresh guacamole. And so do we. We frequent this quaint restaurant where the whole staff speaks Spanish[6] and the food is as authentic as it gets. However, there are also times we've been in a hurry and stopped at Taco Bell. The food is far from authentic; it's

---

[6] At such times, it's nice to have a spouse fluent in Spanish.

handed to us through a window, usually by a young gringo working his way through college; and it's served in paper wrappers or Styrofoam containers. It. Is. Not. Authentic. But know what? It's tasty. Really tasty. It doesn't taste like what we're used to getting at that little Mexican place, but does it need to? It's good, all the same. It's just different. Alas, that "someone" we mentioned—who *knows* good Tex-Mex—would rather do without than eat at Taco Bell.

Pizza is another food that suffers from the "It's different" mentality. We love authentic New York style pizza, and especially from this wonderful Italian restaurant where all the waiters speak broken English to us and Italian to each other. Hey, when in Rome.... But we are not pizza snobs. We'll also eat and enjoy Chicago-style pizza, Dominos take-out, thin and crispy ones from Pizza Hut, and even frozen pizza from the grocery store. Of course, each of these pizza experiences is different, and if we insist on comparing one to another, some of these pizzas are going to come up short. Personally, we don't think a cheap microwave pizza tastes anything like the one we get from our favorite Italian place. But does it need to? As a TV snack, it's not bad at all. *It's just different.*

Different shouldn't automatically translate as "not as good as" or "bad"! Different is … just different. But we live in a world where people are constantly comparing—everything. We compare (and rate) foods, movies, books, ministries, churches and people, to list only a few. And like our maladjusted pooch Misty, when we encounter something that's new or different, something we're not used to, something not like what we were expecting, many of us give it a low score, often needlessly. We compare it to what we know, like, want, and expect; and when we realize it's different, we devalue it and may want nothing more to do with it.

We've listened to ministers who pace the floor and shout, wave their hands and work up a sweat while preaching the Word of God. We've also listened to ministers who stand behind a podium, calmly and softly teaching from the Bible.

And we've heard everything in between. These ministers are different. Do we need to compare them as though they were frozen pizzas? Despite being different, each has something to bring to the table; each presents the Word of God with a unique flavor.

Let's be bold—and fair. Let's approach the different and the unfamiliar with a spirit of adventure—and evaluate every experience based upon its own merits, not on the merits of something or someone else. Don't assume that because "it's different" that it's not as good, especially when dealing with people. Different cultures, different denominations, different ethnicities, different styles, different likes and dislikes. It's all good, even if "it's different." Remember, Jesus said, "Look beneath the surface so you can judge correctly." (John 7:24 NLT)

The Kettle Shrieked at Midnight

THERE'S A NEAT LITTLE directorial trick first used in the 1942 movie *Cat People,* a creepy classic produced by Val Lewton and directed by Jacques Tourneur. Despite its weird title, the movie is actually an intelligent and well-done psychological study of … *oh dear, we're starting to veer off on a tangent.* Anyway, in *Cat People*, there's a suspenseful nighttime sequence in which the film's heroine believes she's being stalked by something on a lonely New York sidewalk.

Cat People, 1942 RKO / Warner Archive

Just as the tension builds to the point viewers think they can't handle anymore, something rushes into the scene with a loud hiss! After we toss our popcorn into the air, we realize it's just a city bus stopping to pick up passengers. This directorial technique came to be known as a "bus"—we hope you can guess why—and it's repeatedly used in movies to make us jump out of our skin. Anything that startles the viewer will work. Sometimes it's the unexpected ring of a telephone piercing the silence, or the wail of a steam locomotive breaking the suspense!

Ever put the kettle on to boil and momentarily forget about it? We have. Once, while waiting to enjoy a cup of tea, we started washing and drying dishes ... and chatting; and *yup*, we forgot all about it. Meanwhile, the water in our kettle was getting hotter and hotter. Pressure built up in the vessel, and when it suddenly vented its steam it *shrieked* at us! Not expecting a "bus" in the kitchen, we almost dropped a couple of plates!

We weren't expecting the peace of our kitchen to be interrupted by a screaming kettle! [7]

And that's the way we all feel when someone we know—possibly even care about—suddenly decides to vent in our direction. If the person is generally a peaceable soul, the sudden outburst can be totally unexpected and it can hurt! If you've been the target of someone venting, a friend, coworker, loved one, and you suffered a steam burn, you can learn the best way to handle such a situation, in the next article, "Cool It!" But for now, we'll discuss how to avoid spouting off at others in the first place.

We understand that sometimes the pressures of life build up in our tiny brains and overtaxed nervous systems, just like water coming to boil in a kettle. And if we've been holding it in, when we finally do vent, through some small outlet—perhaps a friend's normally sympathetic ear —our angst and anxiety erupts like a volcano! Angry words, negative comments, and loud tones spew out like scalding steam.

Physics lesson: why doesn't a saucepan scream at us when it lets off steam? Simple, it has a much larger opening through which to vent, so it's constantly allowing the heat to rise. And hence, there's no internal pressure building up. So pots are peaceful? They *can* be, as we discussed in "Put a Lid on It!," in *Angel in the Kitchen,* the first book in this series.

As people, we usually have one or two confidants to whom we vent. But, sometimes we bottle things up inside, refusing to talk about things that are bothering us, refusing to deal with issues that continue to build tension. Maybe there's a relationship that could benefit from more communication, a situation at work or church that needs to be addressed. Just talk. Don't wait till things are so bad

---

[7] By the way, say hello to Katie Kettle, another of our faithful kitchen angels. Katie graciously agreed to pose for the cover of this book. Thanks, Katie!

that you blow up. Many times, the person who hears us "shriek" isn't even the one who needs to hear what we have to say.

Are you a little hotheaded? You need to cool that down. There's an old expression concerning steam loco-motives: "Build a head of steam"; this is good for trains because it helps them to move forward, but bad for people because it holds us back in just about every human endeavor. So how do we let off more steam more easily and more productively? Glad you asked!

Like the saucepan, we need a larger opening, a larger direction to vent in. That would be God. Hey, He loves it when you vent. He longs to hear every little detail of every problem you're facing. And letting off steam in His direction is much safer and far more productive. First, He always has the answers (which we find by reading His Word daily), and second, once you get it off your chest, you'll be much calmer when you get around the rest of us.

Good advice: Daily vent with the Lord, cool your head and calm your nerves with God's written promises, have the quiet time you need each and every day to avoid letting the cares of life build up inside you. You'll be doing less spouting off, less screaming—and less apologizing. Because, yeah, when you do unexpectedly and accidentally vent, you need to be just as quick to say you're sorry. We've all been there, we all understand about letting off steam, but we need to hear you say it. Okay? Now, how about that cup of tea?

Let all that I am wait quietly before God, for my hope is in him. He alone is my rock and my salvation, my fortress where I will not be shaken. My victory and honor come from God alone. He is my refuge, a rock where no enemy can reach me. O my people, trust in him at all times. Pour out your heart to him, for God is our refuge.

—Psalm 62:5-8 NLT

Cool It!

STEAM BURNS CAN BE BAD. When steam hits flesh, it goes from its gaseous state back to a liquid state. This is a chemical change that releases energy in the form of even more heat. That's why steam cleaning in so effective, and why steam burns are really bad. Steam releases heat that penetrates deep beneath the skin. And it can actually do damage under the surface. On top, the skin is inflamed, but often the wound is much deeper. That's why it's important to apply ice to a steam burn and cool the flesh quickly. Ice soothes, but more importantly, it also dissipates all that heat.

People tend to act like tea kettles. Just as the water in a kettle gets hotter and hotter, building up internal pressure until it finally vents its steam, people frequently allow the pressures of life to build until they can't handle any more—and they suddenly have to vent! They erupt like a raging volcano, spouting scalding emotions and often caustic comments!

Sooner or later we all have volcanic venting, but as we previously explained, our more violent eruptions can be

avoided by "letting off steam" with the Lord, a little each day.

Spend time reading God's Word and talk to the Lord about the pressures you're facing. God longs to hear every little detail of every problem in our lives, and letting off steam in His direction is much safer and far more productive. He always has the answers and once we get things off our chests, we're calmer and better equipped to interact with others.

To avoid spouting off, daily vent with the Lord, cool your head and calm your nerves with God's written promises, have the quiet time you need each day to prevent the pressures of life from building up inside you. But what do you do when someone vents at you?

Yes, steam burns hurt, and the damage often penetrates deep! When people suddenly vent in our direction, the eruption of frustration and anger can be pretty scalding. Anger produces angry words. And misery really does like company, so hurting people often say hurtful things. It's important to remember not to take it personally when someone suddenly vents at you. No, you don't deserve such treatment—who does? But remember, the person has lost emotional control. He or she may say things they don't even mean to say, things they don't even believe to be true, but again, out of stress, frustration, anger, hate, fear, disappointment, jealousy—name your poison—the tongue can become a wicked and deadly weapon!

Try to avoid steam burns in the first place. Never shake a kettle when it's starting to boil inside. That's often the reverse of what people actually do. If they realize something's bothering someone, a coworker, for instance, they will frequently try to stir things up even further. Never poke a hornet's nest with a stick, no matter how long the stick or how fast you can run. Why *would* you, anyway?

If you're minding your own business and still get caught in the blast of someone venting steam, then please remember, *It's not personal!* These things happen. Treat an upset person the same way you'd want to be treated whenever you—and you eventually will—suddenly vent. Do what you can to cool down the situation. "A gentle answer deflects anger, but harsh words make tempers flare." (Proverbs 15:1 NLT)

Sometimes there's absolutely nothing you can say, good or bad, that will help the situation. Sometimes distraught people don't want (or need) to hear your platitudes. In these situations, just keep your mouth shut and wait for the steam to dissipate. Keeping quiet may actually help the person cool off quicker.

Now, not *saying* anything also means that you refrain from communicating non-verbal messages using facial expressions and body language. No smirking, no eye rolling, no Mister-Spock-eyebrow-lifting. Be sympathetic. "Be happy with those who are happy, and weep with those who weep." (Romans 12:15 NLT)

Did you get a steam burn from someone you love, respect, or otherwise care about? Put some ice on it. Quickly, before the heat penetrates more deeply! Cool the hurt and soothe the pain by taking it to the Lord in prayer.

"Come with your wounded spirit! Come with your broken heart! Whatever, then, be your present situation, seek the promised help of the Holy Spirit. He has a healing balm for all...." (John MacDuff, *The Throne of Grace*, 1818-1895)

A Grand Exchange

BEYOND BEING WELL-KNOWN FOODS, what do Swiss chocolate and Brazilian coffee beans have in common? How about Spanish peanuts and California grapes?

None of these foods originated in the regions with which they are most associated. Instead, these foods are all part of "the Grand Exchange" that occurred when Spanish and other European explorers reached the continents of North and South America—a trade of "culinary curiosities" that benefited both the New World and the Old.

When Christopher Columbus "discovered" America in 1492, the great explorer brought with him various grains, fruit trees, and livestock that included sheep and pigs. And when he returned to Spain, he took back such new-found delicacies as sweet potatoes, peanuts and chocolate. Over the next 100 years an incredible and invaluable exchange of food and technology occurred, producing several new industries and bolstering a few sagging economies. During the late 1800s, where would the cowboys of the American Wild West have been had Spanish ships not brought over that four-legged mainstay of Victorian transportation, the horse? And while riding tall in the saddle, what would these "cowpokes" have been herding had European settlers not introduced cattle to North America?

But let's focus on food. We'd hardly be able to call the North American plains "the breadbasket of the world" if wheat, barley and oats hadn't been brought across the sea from the Middle East. Nor would Louisiana have its signature rice, a grain originating in China, had it not been introduced into the New World. And Columbia wouldn't be famous for its coffee beans if the commodity hadn't sailed the Atlantic with a boatload of European insomniacs.

Of course, the gastronomic gifts flowed in both directions in the Grand Exchange: potatoes from Peru eventually became an important part of European diets; and where would all those fabulous Old-World chocolatiers be without the decadent cocoa beans that originated in South America? Ships bound to the Western World from Europe brought bananas, grapes, peaches, pears, olives, turnips, sugarcane, and ... *chickens,* a staple of church dinners and fast-food chains. But in return, these ships carried back the bounty of the Americas, beans, corn, peanuts, pineapples, pumpkins, squash, sweet potatoes, vanilla, and ... *turkeys.* Apparently, all's fowl in love and trade.

Just think, if a ship departed Europe with a cargo of wheat, olives and onions, and it collided with a vessel transporting tomatoes and peppers from South America, you'd have all the ingredients for a really good pizza. A feeble attempt at humor, we agree, but our point here is that the benefits of the Grand Exchange that took place during the 16th century were far greater than the sum of the various parts (or foods). The benefits were a cultural exchange of customs and ideas, and an introduction of new taste sensations previously a world apart.

There's another "grand exchange" that takes place in the spirit realm, when a person becomes a member of the family of God. And like its cultural counterpart, it encompasses a "trade" that's extremely beneficial: our Heavenly Father gives every new believer "beauty for ashes, the oil of joy for mourning, the garment of praise for the spirit of heaviness." (Isaiah 61:3 KJV)

That's quite a trade. It means that God turns our biggest messes into beautiful messages; our greatest tests become our greatest testimonies; situations and circumstances that should have made us bitter end up making us better—or more like Him. Indeed, our Heavenly Father is an expert at turning things around. In fact, He can turn every curse into a blessing. (Deuteronomy 23:5)

We see this in the life of the Biblical hero Joseph. He was wrongly imprisoned (among other things), but his imprisonment eventually led to his vindication, as well as his being installed as the second highest authority in the land of Ancient Egypt. Joseph explains how God made a grand exchange on his behalf: "You intended to harm me, but God intended it all for good. He brought me to this position so I could save the lives of many people." (Genesis 50:20 NLT)

When you feel like you're at the end of your rope; when you're tired, frustrated, and you just don't get it; remember that God knows what you're going through, and He'll trade your weakness for His strength. "That's why I take pleasure in my weaknesses.... For when I am weak, then I am strong." (2 Corinthians 12:10 NLT) If you're going through a tough time, if your life seems a bit messy at present, stop worrying and hand over your problems to the Lord. If you'll trust Him to work on your behalf, He'll turn things around for you. He'll trade you beauty for the ashes of your mistakes, as well as any mistreatment you've suffered.

"And we know God causes everything to work together for the good of those who love Him...." (Romans 8:28 NLT) So, what are you waiting for? Start trading your problems for God's blessings.

The Big Freeze

WE'D LIKE TO INTRODUCE YOU to yet another member of our family of faithful kitchen angels: our upright freezer. Take a bow, Freezer! Freezer? *Ahem.* Sorry, folks, but he prefers to be addressed as *Mister* Freeze! Okay, that's cool. Now say hello to our readers, Mr. Freeze.

Mr. Freeze? Uh, he's not talking today. Please forgive him. Like the famous actor Mr. T, he has a bit of an attitude but, after all, it *is* his nature to be cold.

Mr. Freeze has been with us for quite a few years. He's much older than his cousin, Fridgey. In fact, he's the eldest of his clan, and he'll soon turn 28— *Mr. Freeze!* Be nice. (He doesn't like it when we discuss his age.) Anyway, because Mr. Freeze is an older—excuse us—a "classic" model, he has a habit of quickly accumulating a thick layer of ice on each of his shelves. But as we'll soon explain, this characteristic has come in handy.

Mr. Freeze is a loner, mostly, so he resides in our garage. But he's never totally alone; Mr. Freeze periodically hangs out with our blue SUV. That is, when Blue isn't running the road. And at night, while we sleep, these two faithful servants share stories. Blue usually has the most exciting tales to relate, hair-raising adventures of the freeway and ... *well....*

Mr. Freeze has his own share of legends to relate, and one night he—

What's that? Okay. Mr. Freeze wants to tell the story:

It was a dark and stormy night ... and all through the house, not a creature was stirring—except this one goofy mouse.

That was way back in 1999, during the early morning hours of Christmas Eve. While my friends Tom and Wilma snoozed, a massive ice storm moved over the southeast and dropped several inches of freezing rain. (Grrr, what a show-off!)

My friends awoke to the sounds of tree branches breaking under the weight of a thick coating of ice. (The nerve! I make the ice around here!) Anyway, there were downed power lines everywhere, and Woodhaven didn't have electricity for ten days. But did Tom and Wilma's food go bad? Not while I'm on the job!

Sure, I didn't have any power either, but I'm well insulated; and my layers of ice kept things good and cold—just like a big camping cooler! Everything that needed refrigeration I kept nice and fresh! Hey, Fridgey, did ya hear that?

Um, we all heard it, Mr. Freeze. But yes, it's true, you saved the day. You're a hero, a true legend in the annals of kitchen history. And because you're an elder appliance, you deserve our respect and admiration.

By the way, some people are just like Mr. Freeze: they come across as cold (and distant). When we get around these people, they tend to give us a frosty reception (they're grumpy). But like Mr. Freeze, they've endured many storms in life. Their outlook and emotions have been chilled by hurts and disappointments; and they've built up protective layers to insulate themselves from the world. Many of them have become as cold and hardened as pack ice.

Jesus warns us, "Because lawlessness will multiple, the love of many will grow cold." (Matthew 24:12 HCS) In other words, the chill of our hurts and disappointments can cause pain, resentment, distrust, unforgiveness, and even a general feeling of bitterness to accumulate like layers of ice around our hearts. We can eventually become much like the shelves within Mr. Freeze: bound by "ice" and frozen in life.

It's easy to turn and walk away from people who are hurting and "iced up." Because, as author and speaker Joyce Meyer often states, "Hurting people hurt people." But the Mister and Missus Freezes of this world nevertheless need our help, as well as the thawing influence of genuine love. King Solomon wrote, "Love is as strong as death.... [It] flashes like fire.... Many waters cannot quench love...." (Song of Solomon 8:6-7 NLT)

Love is the most powerful force in the universe; and God's love is life's universal antifreeze. 1 Corinthians 13 describes its "composition." When we apply it, God's supernatural Agape Love allows us to endure a little frostbite and eventually break through the ice that insulates people. God's love allows us to look beyond bad attitudes and nasty dispositions. It enables our Lord to use us to melt the coldest heart.

So drop the ice pick and put down the tongs, because "Love never fails." (1 Corinthians 13:8 ISV)

The Big Thaw

WE HAVE FURTHER ADVENTURES to share about our faithful upright freezer, that legend among our kitchen angels who, please remember, wishes to be addressed as *Mister Freeze.*

Because Mr. Freeze is an old model—excuse us, we did promise to never discuss his age—a *classic* model, he tends to accumulate thick layers of ice on all his shelves and cooling coils. As we mentioned in "The Big Freeze," this frosty characteristic of our tireless servant once came in handy, when we lost power for days: Mr. Freeze had so much ice built up that he was able to keep things well chilled until the power was restored. (He loves for us to tell this story.)

But there are times when too much ice is...well, too much. The buildup of ice on Mr. Freeze's coils drastically reduces his efficiency. Hence, it takes more power for him to function properly—and actually, with all that ice chok-ing his coils, he's really *not* functioning properly.

Another downside of his icy condition is that eventually things no longer fit in his iced-up compartments. What was once a 12-inch clearance can easily become a nine-inch clearance, because his shelves are bound in about 3 inches of freezer frost. That's when it's time to stop writing and give Mr. Freeze a little TLC in the form of defrosting. Or as he describes it, "The Big Thaw." (We really should stop let-ting Mr. Freeze watch all those old detective movies.)

The Big Thaw is, quite honestly, a big mess. As the ice slowly melts away, all sorts of things reveal themselves: locked within the thick layers of freezer frost are the memories of foods long gone. Funky odors are emitted, which Mr. Freeze finds a little embarrassing. Strange stains of purple, orange or red sometimes surface, probably from tiny leaks of concentrated fruit juices or the occasional drop of blood from a sirloin; along with bits of soggy cardboard from old packages, preserved like fossils in a tar pit; and endless puddles of cloudy water that collect on the garage floor, requiring towels and old newspapers galore.

Mr. Freeze stands there with his door wide open, feeling a little exposed, as chunks of long-accumulated ice fall away from his neglected coils, and all his dirty little secrets drain away.... *Ahem.* But it's all for the best. Afterwards, Mr. Freeze feels like a new appliance, running smoothly and once again ready to tackle the world of frozen foods.

Can you relate to Mr. Freeze? Are your spiritual coils choked by the ice of emotional wounds or indiscretion? Is the frost of past failures clogging areas of your life, until there's no room for new people, new directions, and new dreams?

As we go through life we tend to accumulate thick layers of "ice": hurts and disappointments start to cool our fervor; unforgiveness can chills our hearts; and before we know it, we're bound by the ice, separated from God and others by a thick layer of frost. When that happens, it's time for the Big Thaw.

We need to open our hearts to God—wide open, like Mr. Freeze's door—and allow the Holy Spirit and the Word of God to defrost our attitudes and our relationships. David's continual prayer was "Create a clean heart in me, O God, and renew a faithful spirit within me." (Psalm 51:10 GW)

As our guilt and burdens melt away, we'll detect the rotten stench of any bitterness and unforgiveness, see bits of soggy "cardboard" from our past mistakes, and the stains of old sins at last confronted. That icy heaviness will begin to fall away, leaving us free once again, and functioning more smoothly and efficiently.

...Let us lay aside every weight, and sin which clings so closely, and let us run with endurance the race... before us.
—Hebrews 12:1 ESV

The Cookie Jar

DO YOU HAVE A COOKIE JAR in your kitchen?

Cookie jars were first used in England toward the end of the 18th century—only they were called biscuit barrels. These containers were usually simple glass jars with metal lids. However, tea biscuits were frequently sold in metal containers and these "biscuit tins" were often saved and reused.

For some reason, cookie jars started becoming popular in the United States during the Great Depression, which started in 1929. Perhaps people were feeling these common household containers were a safer place to stash their hard-earned nickels and dimes. Around this time, cylindrical-shaped stoneware cookie jars, many of which were decorated with a floral pattern, began to replace the simpler, plain glass jars.

vintage biscuit tin

A few years later, the Brush Pottery Company of Ohio produced the first cookie jars made of ceramic, a material which allowed the containers to be molded into a variety of shapes, such as fruits, vegetables, animals or comical figures. Suddenly people were collecting cookie jars, and several companies decided to encourage the craze by offering a seemingly endless array of designs—ushering in a "golden age" of American cookie jar production, from 1940 until the early 1970s.

We have a beautiful "birdhouse" cookie jar on our kitchen counter—because we love birds!—and we store our Pepperidge Farm Milano cookies inside it. We buy these delicious cookies to keep on hand in case any guests drop by unexpectedly; we want to always have a treat to serve them with their coffee. So we don't usually pilfer the cookie jar. In fact, we keep the bag of Milano cookies sealed until we need them. We only eat them ourselves if they're close to going out of date, after we've replaced them with a fresh pack. We're good like that.

Wish we could say the same were true of us when we were kids. Both of us were frequently "caught with our hand in the cookie jar"! Wilma's mom had a Mother Goose cookie jar. Tom's mother had a teddy bear cookie jar. Both jars were kept well stocked. Both jars were an endless source of red-faced shame: there's something embarrassing about being caught standing tippy-toed on a kitchen chair with one hand fishing around inside the head of a brown ceramic bear. *Busted!*

The phrase "caught with your hand in the cookie jar" means: to be discovered taking something you're not entitled to. When it comes to cookies, there may be several reasons we're not entitled to a cookie: we're saving the cookies for guests; we're dieting and don't need a cookie; we've already had our fair share of cookies; it's close to dinner and we'll spoil our appetites. Phooey! When you're a kid, none of this seems fair. We just want a cookie!

"Hand in the cookie jar" has another, informal meaning: to take advantage of one's unique position by accepting favors. For instance, "That public official has his hand in the cookie jar."

As believers, we have a unique position in Jesus Christ: we are the sons and daughters of God—His children—and we're also the Lord's ambassadors here on earth. And know what? In His "celestial kitchen," our Heavenly Father has His own "cookie jar"! It's shaped like a "lamb without spot or wrinkle," and it's called God's abundant life and blessings. He keeps it well stocked, and we never have to fear being caught with our hand in the cookie jar, because His blessings are there especially for us—not just for special guests. Anyone can reach in and grab an "abundant life biscuit" or indulge in a "double stuff" blessing.

Our Heavenly Father is always generous with His cookie jar, and He wants us to help ourselves to as many cookies as we want. "[God] withholds no good thing from those who have integrity." (Psalm 84:11 NET Bible) His supply of blessings never runs out, and besides, He trusts us to share whatever we receive—instead of acting like the Cookie Monster. "Blessed be the Lord, who daily loads us with benefits." (Psalm 68:19 KJ2000)

Cookies whenever we want one? Hey, our Heavenly Father is not just an "eat your vegetables" God. He wants us to enjoy our days, so He always keeps the cookie jar in easy reach, 24/7—365 days a year. So have *another* cookie.

Jesus said, "...If you sinful people know how to give good gifts to your children, how much more will your heavenly Father give good gifts to those who ask him." (Matthew 7:11 NLT)

Magic with Leftovers

WE HAVE A WONDERFUL COOKBOOK in our collection, titled *Magic with Leftovers*. It was published in 1955 and contains over 300 recipes for turning the remnants of our meals of yesterday (and perhaps the day before) into something fresh and new. One such recipe is for a chef salad that makes use of whatever meats you happen to find in the fridge—and not just the usual salad ingredient of ham.

Personally, we like to cook up stir fry using leftover meats and veggies, which we serve over a bed of fluffy rice. And while we're discussing stir fry, here's some trivia for you: chop suey was created in America by Chinese immigrants ... using leftovers! The name of the dish actually comes from the Chinese *tsap seui*, which translates "miscellaneous leftovers." According to legend, several tough-looking and half-starved customers walked into a Wild West saloon circa 1890, demanding food. The saloon had been busy that day, and had run out of steaks and stew. The poor Chinese cook was too scared to break the bad news to this pack of intimidating cowpokes, so he quickly threw whatever he could find into his wok: bits of leftover meats and vegetables. He quickly fried these remnants and served them up to his enthusiastic diners.

When asked what the wonderful dish was called, the cook didn't lie. He nervously responded, miscellany—only in Chinese. The words came out, "Chop suey!" But this savvy chef had turned leftovers from a long day of serving breakfast, lunch and dinner into something magical. Nice ending, right? However, we don't want to know exactly where he found these leftovers.

Okay, when it comes to food, leftovers can be magical, but when it comes to our relationship with God, there's nothing magical about giving Him our leftovers. And yet, that's exactly what we often do; we serve up to our Heavenly Father whatever's left over of our day, after we've already consumed the best parts of our time, energy and talents.

It's usually only after we've worked and played, after we're worn out and the day's almost done, that many of us decide to toss a little something to the Lord. It's often not even as appetizing as the impromptu chop suey served up at the end of the day by that hapless Chinese cook: a half-numb and, hence, halfhearted prayer of Thanks, God. Please watch over me while I sleep. before slumber claims the one praying.

King David, the prolific poet and giant-slayer, the busy warrior and the writer of the Psalms—the most encouraging words ever penned—once wrote "...Thou art my God; early will I seek Thee; my soul thirsteth for Thee...." (Psalm 63:1 KJV) King David was telling his Lord that, before scheduling or doing anything else, he would spend time with God; that he would make Him the Number One Priority.

Not keeping God as our first priority in everything is hazardous to our spiritual health. We must always seek to do His will, not ours; and ensure that we spend quality time with Him. He deserves more than our leftovers: three minutes here, two minutes there. And since it's so easy to get busy and then run out time, it's best to schedule God into your first hour of the day—before you go for a jog, or make breakfast; before you get the kids off to school; before you check your email or watch the news. Before you meet the challenges of the day, first meet with the God who created the day.

Don't fool yourself that you'll do it later. "Later" never comes. And the "enemy of your soul" will do everything in his power to keep you too busy, and to distract you from reading the Bible and praying to the Lord of ALL—from spending quality time with your Heavenly Father.

Don't serve God your leftovers. He is loving and gracious, and He's willing to take whatever we give Him. Indeed, He's able to take our leftover time and talents and cook up something *magical* with them. But He does this in a pinch, like the Chinese cook. Imagine what God could do with a prime cut of your day? Please, stop throwing God your scraps. After all, He never gives us *His* leftovers!

Leftovers Again?!?

GETTING BACK TO FOOD, leftovers *can* be delicious.

We actually look forward to leftovers. After all, if it was good the first time around, why wouldn't it be tasty the second time? And some dishes, such as Puerto Rican rice and beans (from a secret recipe Wilma's mom taught her), are actually better after they've had time to "rest" overnight in the fridge. All the seasonings seem to rally for another round of culinary adventure. That's why we make extra: so we can have more (!); and also to save time, by cooking one meal that feeds us over the course of about three nights. Waste not, want not.

But not everyone likes leftovers. In fact, we have a good friend who refuses to eat leftovers. He grew up in extreme poverty, and leftovers were all he ever had to eat—and by "leftovers," we don't mean a cold drumstick from a turkey feast. Fortunately, our friend is married to a very understanding lady who loves to cook and doesn't mind serving up something different at every meal. She gets the "Kitchen Saint" Award.

Speaking of drumsticks, there's one time of year that almost no one—at least not here in the U.S.—says *no* to leftovers, and it comes around on the fourth Thursday of every November.

After observing the great feast of Thanksgiving, a day on which most of us cook way too much food, and end up as stuffed as the turkey, people really start getting creative with all the leftovers. They may have a sliced turkey sandwich while watching the big game, or try to eat lighter the next day by having a salad with diced turkey. And then there's chipped turkey on toast, creamed turkey on rice, turkey omelets, turkey casseroles, turkey soup, turkey stew, turkey *turkey*.... Excuse us, but does anyone have an antacid handy?

Eventually everyone gets sick and tired of turkey, and the "magic" of leftovers loses its ... *well*, magic. In life, also, "leftovers" grow tiresome and can quickly drain the magic from our relationships with friends and family.

Oftentimes, a person gives so much time and energy to a project at work, or to building a career or running a ministry, that he or she has very little left for the people closest to them. Instead of serving those closest to them with love, patience and encouragement, they instead dish out what's left over at the end of a hard day: grumpiness, defensiveness, and possibly even outbursts of anger.

Today there are far too many neglected spouses and children who are sick and tired of getting the "leftovers." They resent seeing their husband or wife or mom or dad play the role of Mr. or Ms. Wonderful while in public, when behind closed doors they are anything but wonderful. And the excuses of work stress and fatigue soon grow old. Leftovers are still leftovers, no matter what the reason.

Some parents make up for giving their kids the leftovers by buying them "expensive desserts"; but kids want attention, not toys. They need their moms and dads, not their purses. Word of advice to parents: don't toss your kids the leftovers of your time and energy. If you do, you may be in for a surprise: as you grow older, your kids may start giving you *their* leftovers. (Psalm 127:3)

Having problems in your marriage? Could it be because you're serving your spouse the leftovers? Or maybe the demands of life have caused *both* of you to serve leftovers to the other. Examine the state of affairs—*honestly*—and then do your utmost to give your spouse the *best* you have to offer. Like you did when you were dating. Remember?

Guys, when was the last time you brought home (or sent) flowers to your wife? Or gave her a pretty card—just because? When was the last time you told her how much you love and appreciate her? Do you make her feel like a princess? The Apostle Paul writes, "Husbands, love your wives, just as Christ loved the Church and gave Himself up for her." (Ephesians 5:25 NIV)

Ladies, when was the last time you made your husband his favorite meal, or sent *him* a card—just because? When was the last time you told him how much you love and appreciate him? Do you make him feel like he's your hero? The Apostle Paul also writes, "Wives should respect their husbands." (Ephesians 5:22 GW)

Take inventory. Are your friends and family lamenting, "What, leftovers *again*?" Sooner or later, people get tired of receiving only the dregs of our time, talents and energies. When it comes to relationships, there's nothing magical about leftovers.

Beware of the Blob!

LONG AFTER MIDNIGHT, while watching a creepy classic on the late-late movie, we see it: a scene so hideous in its simple truth, so horrifying that—- We shudder and try to look away, but it's too late! And now, we may never be able to fully purge the sickening image from our fevered brains!

The scene: in a dimly-lit kitchen a woman is removing what appears to be an ordinary cookie sheet from her oven. Unbeknownst to her, however, a strange alien substance has covered the cookie sheet; an evil, slimy film that's been lurking there ... awaiting the right moment to strike.

The nasty stuff begins to grow ... rising, taking on a ghoulish shape. It's grey and gooey, sticky and scarier than anything we've seen before!

Wait a minute, we cry in unison. Are we watching a repeat of *The Blob* with Steve McQueen? Remember that 1958 sci-fi flick? Hapless viewers were warned by the movie's opening theme song, "Beware of the blob! It creeps; And leaps, and glides and slides; Across the floor; Right through the door; And all around the wall—A splotch, a blotch! Be careful of the blob!" Corny? Hey, watch it. The great pop composer Burt Bacharach wrote those crazy lyrics.

All this aside, we were absolutely wrong. Guess our minds wandered a moment, and we hadn't realized we were now watching a commercial for Pam Cooking Spray. You know, the stuff that keeps food from sticking to pots, pans, and baking surfaces.

Image from a commercial for ConAgra's Pam Cooking Spray.

Apparently, the lady in the commercial had forgotten to spray on the Pam, and now the thin residue of old food, which clung tenaciously to her cookie sheet, was rising up to expose her mistake. "I am the ghost of meals past," it proclaims, ready to haunt her taste buds with the disgusting flavors of meals long gone but not quite forgotten.

Imagine, a funky residue of spinach quiche invading the taste of your chocolate chip cookies. Nothing ruins the enjoyment of a good cookie more than something nasty-tasting mingling with the butter and brown sugar. Yuck!

By the way, life is like a cookie sheet. No, really. In life, we make mistakes; we encounter conflicts and disappointments; and in our relationships we experience, at one time or another, hurts, misunderstandings, and even betrayals. Sometimes the pain and disillusionment of the past lingers on. It sticks to us like that gooey glob in the Pam commercial. We think we've moved on, but a thin film of nasty experiences sticks to our hearts. It's those memories that leave a "bad taste" in our mouths—months, even years, later. These "ghosts" can continue to haunt us, with emotional "residue" that can contaminate fresh relationships and new experiences, preventing us from fully tasting all the good things in life.

Why do bad things seem to stick, even long after we "forgive and forget"? Well, with God, forgiveness and acceptance are instant. The Bible states, "God is faithful and reliable. If we confess our sins, He forgives them and cleanses us from everything we've done wrong." (1 John 1:9 GW)

There's no residue of the past, because nothing sticks. The cookie sheet of our lives is left clean as a whistle. And our loving, merciful Heavenly Father does not bring up the past to mess up the "flavor" of our present. Instead, He casts "all our sins into the depths of the sea." (Micah 7:19 JUB). In other words, He scours the "pan" and then flushes the residue down the drain.

Alas, if only people could do the same. Being weak and fallen creatures (say "humans"), we tend to cling to our hurts and disappointments. This partly stems from self-righteousness. Ouch! We all make mistakes, and we've all let someone down in the past. But we refuse to consider the old proverb, "To err is human, to forgive divine." So we need to give those who hurt us a break. After all, they're only human. Spray on the PAM of love and forgiveness. "For Love covers a multitude of sins." (1 Peter 4:8 NLT)

We need to cut ourselves some slack, too. Some emotional wounds do take time to heal. And yet, even after forgiving ourselves and others—and moving forward—we may still feel some emotional residue. But that's where God comes into the picture. He is like spiritual PAM!

As we grow closer to God, we become more like Him. We begin to see things the way He sees them, and we begin to respond the way God would respond. As we mature in the Lord, we are better able to overcome hurts and disappointments. We get better at forgiving, and better at going through life without having every insult and injury stick to us.

We can only truly forgive and move forward when we include God in the process. So, be honest with your Heavenly Father. Present your hurts to Him in prayer. "Give all your worries and cares to God, for he cares about you." (1 Peter 5:7 NLT) Ask Him to scrape away any emotional residue, to give you a divine perspective, and cover you with His love.

A little spiritual PAM will keep you free from those ugly emotional blobs that come creeping and crawling—and which try to cling to the heart. Don't get stuck. Be free. Free from being haunted by the ghosts of past mistakes, hurts, and disappointments. Free to taste the good things God has prepared for you. (Ephesians 2:10)

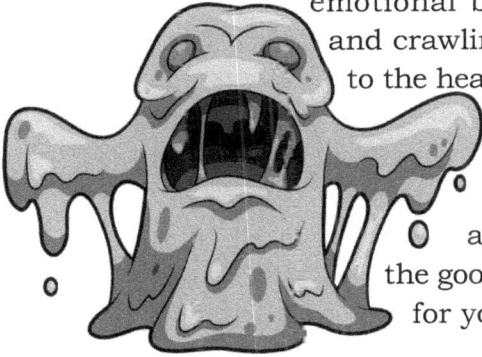

The Wisdom of an Egg

EVER NOTICED HOW OFTEN people use eggs to illustrate a point? For instance, "he's a good egg—but she's a rotten egg." And how about: "the yolks on you"? Or, "you can't unscramble eggs"?

We hope you can relate, because if you can't, then as writers, we'll end up with egg all over our faces. Yes, eggs seem to have much to teach us, which makes them true angels (messengers) in the kitchen.[8]

One thing we recently learned about this dynamic dietary darling with the Humpty-Dumpty body, came to us while watching a cooking show on TV. The show's chef explained that there's a "right" way to crack an egg. Oh

---

[8] See *Angel in the Kitchen* for more egg wisdom.

really?!? And all this time we'd been thinking you just smack the sucker against the edge of a bowl.

Nope. The right way to crack an egg is on a flat surface, such as the kitchen counter. If you crack the egg on the rim of a bowl, the chef explained, pieces of the shell are pushed into the egg white. These shell fragments usually end up in the mixing bowl, and have to be picked out by hand—*if* you spot them. So if you don't want tiny, gritty chips of calcium in your cakes or soufflés, then gently crack the eggs against a flat surface.

Now that's kitchen wisdom. But the egg has far more to teach us. Call it "egg wisdom." In fact, if you "egg" us on, we'll share a nugget ... or two ... or three. Actually, we'll share it even if you don't egg us on.

Ready? "Don't put all your eggs into one basket."

We all know what this old saying means, but how many of us know where it came from? Seriously, why eggs? Why not "don't put all your milk in one jug"? Or something else like that? Well, we'll tell you.

We were losing sleep over this one, so we just had to know. After researching the oft-used idiom, we learned that it first appeared in the classic Spanish novel *Don Quixote*. But not really. Confused?

In Miguel de Cervantes' novel, originally published in two parts (in 1605 and 1615), Sancho Panza proclaims, "It is the part of a wise man to keep himself today for tomorrow, and not venture all his eggs in one basket." Faithful Sancho is sharing wisdom about the decisions we make today, and about our plans for the future. But did Cervantes really coin the famous phrase? Not quite. At the time, there was no such idiom in the Spanish language.

The great writer did pen a line expressing the same

meaning, but the actual phrase "don't put all your eggs in one basket" is the handiwork of a British book editor, who got a bit too creative while preparing a later, English-translation edition of the novel. This liberal-minded editor may have picked up the idiom from an Italian source, because in 1662, the popular book Italian Proverbial Phrases listed the following entry: "To put all ones Eggs in a Paniard, *viz.* to hazard all in one bottom."

A paniard is similar to a saddlebag, but the word is derived from the Latin *panarium* (or bread basket). To "hazard" all your eggs "in one bottom" is to place all your hopes and dreams, all your ideas and interests, all your money and resources, all your plans—all your whatever—in a single area or activity. Then, if the bottom should fall out (literally or figuratively), all your "eggs" will drop to the ground, crack open, and be ruined. On the other hand, putting your eggs into several different baskets insures some will remain intact. After all, what are the odds of two or more baskets all having bad bottoms?

Applying to a college or for a job? Egg wisdom advises you send out multiple applications and/or résumés. If you receive a *no* regarding one, then simply move on to the next opportunity. Pursuing a dream? Explore several avenues. If you hit a brick wall, then simply try another way. Never give up. One rejection, one dead end, one nasty naysayer, one bottomless "basket" is *not* the end.

Investing? Read on.

The sound advice we've dubbed *egg wisdom* is actually scriptural in origin. The Biblical King Solomon wrote, "Send your resources out over the seas; eventually you will reap a return. Divide your merchandise into seven or eight shares, since you don't know what disasters may come on the earth." (Ecclesiastes 11:1-2, CJB) Notice the use of the plural: *seas*, not *sea*. Solomon further admonishes us to split up our resources into multiple lots.

When he wrote this passage, the wisest of Israel's kings was giving advice in regard to both giving and investing, because—thanks to the divine law of reciprocity—the two actions are indeed linked. When we give of our time, talents and resources, and with the proper motives (always out of love), we are investing in the lives of others. Indeed, Luke states "Give, and you will receive. A large quantity, pressed together, shaken down, and running over will be put into your pocket...." (Luke 6:38 GW)

All this aside, we just wanted you to know that when Solomon advised his people to "divide" their resources, he was essentially saying, "Don't put all your eggs into one basket." He just needed a British book editor who'd been reading Latin proverbs.

So, mystery solved: our first bit of egg wisdom comes from the source of all wisdom, the timeless Word of God.

Before they Hatch

EGGS TEND TO GET MIXED into just about everything: cakes, cookies, and pies; quiches, puddings, and soufflés; meatloaf and meatballs; and even protein shakes.

Of course, the biggest egg mash-ups occur at breakfast, or brunch, when various ingredients are mixed to create an omelet. Most people think of these as a simple blend of eggs and milk (or a little cream), salt and pepper, and maybe some shredded cheese. But when the omelet gets fancy, and the eggs go cavorting with onions, peppers, mushrooms, tomatoes and other ingredients, cooks and restaurants love to call the resultant concoction a Spanish omelet. Sorry, but this, however, is incorrect.

Perhaps these confused cooks are simply paying homage to the dish that inspired this culinary creation, but more likely they've mixed up two similar but distinct egg dishes. What's actually being served by these cooks is a Western-style or Mexican omelet. We write this with a good bit of authority, and can safely state that a true Spanish omelet resembles a quiche and has potatoes baked inside of it. It's called a *Tortilla Española*. To further the confusion, in the U.S. a "tortilla" is a piece of Mexican flat bread used to wrap meats, cheese, and veggies.

In the same way we love to mash, mix, and blend our eggs—as well as our egg recipes—many of us have a habit of mashing, mixing and blending famous expressions or figures of speech. These "word omelets" are called *malaphors*.

A malaphor is a mashup of two idioms, which results when someone confuses two similar figures of speech. The resulting expression usually makes no sense at all. For instance, we once overheard an old friend describing the good fortune of one of his coworkers, by commenting "He came out smelling like a bandit." *Hm.* Is that good or bad? We're not sure if bandits bathe or even bother with deodorant. But we're reasonably certain our friend had mixed two similar expressions, intending to say his coworker either "came out smelling like a rose" or "made out like a bandit."

Speaking of mixing up eggs and egg recipes, here's a mixing of two well-known egg idioms. "Don't count your eggs before they hatch." This is an omelet—*er*, malaphor—blending two eggs-pressions. Actually, a better piece of advice would be "Don't count your *chickens* before they hatch" But unlike many malaphors, this one is used frequently (if erroneously) and it still makes perfect sense.

Have you ever seen a bird protecting its nest? Each time the mama bird has to briefly fly away, upon returning, she appears to be examining and counting her eggs. If one's missing the mother will put up a squawk. Partly because she has potentially lost a baby bird, but also because ... after all, that's generally the sound birds make.

It's a sad fact of life, however, that not all of those eggs are guaranteed to hatch. Having seven eggs is no guarantee of getting seven baby birds. Likewise, having a job offer is no guarantee you'll be able to pay the bills at the end of the month. So don't stop sending out résumés and going on job interviews.

And if you get a letter from Publisher's Clearing House stating you've potentially won some big prizes, don't run out to spend the money until it's safely in the bank. In fact, wait till the check has cleared. In life, at least where people and institutions are concerned, you usually can't count on something—and depend upon it—until it comes to pass. The same can be said of all our intricate planning, also, because the future is uncertain.

It's totally human, of course, to be "hatching a scheme" at any given moment, whether it's in the pursuit of a goal or a dream, or in trying to achieve great things in a business, a ministry, or an avocation. But as the great poet Robert Burns once wrote, "the best laid plans of mice and men often go awry."

So we should never count our eggs before they hatch. But what happens when we do count on something and it falls through? Well, instead of benefitting from something that takes flight, we've just (as the saying goes) laid an egg. (Wow, it's really hard to get away from the egg analogy.)

Sigh! Isn't there anything in life we can count on?

When it comes to Spiritual matters, it's okay to count on God's blessings and promises. In fact, our Heavenly Father wants us to count each and every one of these "eggs" as though they've already hatched, taken flight, and even flown the coop.

God wants us to have faith (complete trust) in Him, His Word, His promises, and His ability to answer prayer. "Now faith is the assurance (the confirmation, the title deed) of the things [we] hope for, being the proof of things [we] do not see and the conviction of their reality [faith perceiving as real fact what is not revealed to the senses]." (Hebrews 11:1 AMP) Faith, is the spiritual, supernatural, God-approved version of counting your chickens *before* they hatch.

When it comes to prayer and God's promises, our Heavenly Father wants us to view life with our "spiritual eyes"— seeing by faith and counting on the results and benefits (our spiritual eggs) before such things come to fruition (hatch). Faith is having confidence in God to deliver what He's promised, no matter how long the process takes, or how difficult the situation.

Things may look or sound pretty bad, according to our human senses, but the Apostle Paul admonishes all believers to "walk by faith, not by sight." (2 Corinthians 5:7 KJV)

Spiritual mumbo-jumbo? Hardly. Even motivational experts, speaking to corporate employees in regards to success, support the ideas behind this ancient Biblical principle. In their 2003 book *Chicken Soup for the Soul: Living Your Dreams,* writers Jack Canfield and Mark Victor Hanson state, "One of the secrets to success is to start acting like a success before you are one."

The two men go on to ask, "If you had already achieved your dream.... How would you act?"

As believers we are to act according to how we see ourselves through the eyes of faith. We may not look it, but we are loved, accepted, welcomed, and saved. And we are a complete success in Jesus Christ. Even when things don't go as planned, even when we make mistakes, we can have confidence that God will see us through. (Correction: He has *already* seen us through.)

By faith you *can*—and *should*—count your Spiritual eggs before they hatch. You'll be doing *eggs-actly* as God desires. No *eggs-aggeration*.

Eggshells: The Inside Story

YOU CAN'T JUDGE A BOOK by its cover. Nor can you tell if an egg is fresh by examining its shell.

Although the wisdom is the same in both cases, the consequences of neglecting it in the former are by far preferable to the latter. Allow us to explain: if you crack a book with an interesting title and a cool cover illustration, but then realize it's pretty bad ... you can always take a good nap. But if you crack open an innocent-looking egg and realize it's rotten ... well, you'll be fumigating the house.

The shell of an egg is composed mostly of calcium carbonate, and remains unblemished and smooth to the touch long after the yolk inside has gone bad. In fact, the egg can be decomposing inside while the shell can appear enticingly fresh. Good thing we've all learned not to form conclusions based on appearances alone. Right?

We never crack an egg directly into something we're mixing, such as a cake mix. If it's bad, it's also too bad—because it's too late to do anything about it. Hence, we break each egg into a separate bowl, and examine it before adding it to the recipe. When eggs go bad, the whites start to look watery. The yolks darken and may appear slightly shriveled. Of course, if the egg is rotten you'll know the moment you crack it.

Refrigerated eggs tend to have a long shelf-life, usually a month beyond their sell-by date. But eggs that were mishandled and subjected to high temperatures go bad more quickly. Bad eggs can breed life-threatening bacteria, so it's best to know what's lurking beneath those pretty shells. But how can you tell?

There's a simple test. Does the egg float in a deep bowl of water, or sink to the bottom? No, this isn't similar to the lunacy of dunking would-be witches centuries ago. This is based on science, not superstition.

First, every egg contains a tiny pocket of air. You can see where this air pocket formed, whenever you peel a boiled egg: the larger end of the boiled egg will always be flat and dimpled. As an egg ages, this air pocket expands, which increases its buoyancy. A fresh egg doesn't contain enough air to float. It will sink to the bottom of the bowl and lie on its side.

Second, as eggs age the yolks produce gases. If the egg sinks but remains "standing" on one end, then gases are forming at the other end. It's still okay to use the egg, but don't dawdle about it. If, however, the egg floats, then a considerable pocket of gases has formed—indicating the egg is well on its way to rotting.

Bad eggs produce hydrogen sulfide, which builds within the shell. This foul-smelling gas is an indication of the corruption taking place within a shell that appears perfect on the outside, smooth and unblemished. Thank goodness, though, we don't have to judge an egg by its shell.

As we've stated before, people are like eggs. Yes, there are good eggs, bad eggs, and rotten eggs; but our point here is that we can never base our judgements on appearance alone. A person who looks fine, and who seems to have it altogether, may actually be "dying" on the inside.

Unfortunately, in our Western culture we tend to value outer beauty above inner beauty, and physical perfection above strength of character. Many of us see the outer success, fame, and fortune of celebrity athletes and movie stars, and then assume their private lives are just as rich and wonderful. Occasionally, however, we'll read or hear about a rich and famous person who's been battling with the inner demons of addiction, physical abuse, low self-esteem, and ... emptiness. In fact, we can recall one such celebrity confessing that, by all appearances, he had "made it" in life and had everything he could possibly desire—except happiness.

Since the lifestyles of the rich and famous, like eggshells, can conceal foul feelings and serious problems, it's important we don't make assumptions based on appearances. This wisdom has a spiritual application, too—one many of us seldom consider—which is the reverse of our egg analogy.

You may know someone who doesn't look or dress or act like a star; but probably inside the shell of the "ugly duckling" there resides a beautiful, talented, or well-adjusted "swan"! And perhaps you know an older person who's grown grey and wrinkled and stooped; perhaps a "senior saint" within your faith community; someone who appears to be years beyond his or her "best-by" date. The shell may look a little worse for wear, but you might just be surprised at how much life still resides within. Never discount what these people have to offer.

The Apostle Paul wrote, "Though our outer self is heading for decay, our inner self is being renewed daily." (2 Corinthians 4:16 CJB) Or, to quote the Phillips translation, "The outward man does indeed suffer wear and tear, but every day the inward man receives fresh strength. ...For we are looking all the time not at the visible things but at the invisible.

The visible things are transitory: it is the invisible things that are really permanent [eternal]." (2 Corinthians 4:16-18)

Perhaps no one is ever *eggs-actly* as he or she appears. "Beautiful eggs" may be dying inside. Apparent good eggs can stink. Dull and pathetic-looking eggs can be full of life. And alleged "bad eggs" may still turn out to be good. Let's try to see beyond the shells.

I look to a day when people will not be judged by the color of their skin, but by the content of their character.
—Dr. Martin Luther King, Jr.

Short-Sighted in the Kitchen

BY NOW MOST OF OUR dear readers surely must realize we're a few bucks shy of being certifiably eccentric. Given our present financial state, please refer to us as simply daffy. True, we give our kitchen appliances names, and then write about the adventures of these "angels." And again, we call them angels because, like God's celestial messengers, these kitchen tools and appliances generally have a life-changing lesson to impart—*if* we look for it.

In the first book in this series, we introduced Luke and Nuke, the identical microwave ovens residing in our home. Having microwave twins now allows us to fix *two* bags of popcorn simultaneously, and.... Uh, hang on, we didn't actually *have* microwave twins—we bought them. At a home-improvement store. Honest. After all, you can have a headache but you can't have a microwave—not even if you're listed in *The Guinness Book of World Records*. Ahem, moving on....

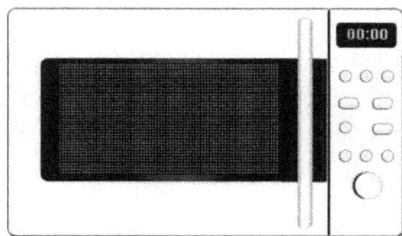

Luke and Nuke have their own little rooms, so to speak. They reside in two compartments located among the kitchen cabinets—well above the countertop—because one of us is a stickler for keeping the counters free of clutter.

I'm LUKE! *He's* Nuke. Can't you see the difference between us?!

(*Note: I'm pleased to say, that would be me. —-Wilma*)

From their "perches" Luke and Nuke survey the scene below, quietly watching, awaiting our every quick-cooking need. A good thing, too, because we recently had to call upon them to cook two frozen mini-pizzas.

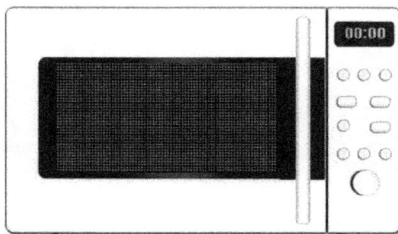

I'm NUKE! *He's* Luke. I'm better looking and more talented!

The instructions on the box stated: "place pizza on top of carton, then place carton into microwave." We did this—twice—and 90 seconds later Luke and Nuke beeped us that it was snack time.

Later, Wilma wiped out the insides of both microwaves using an all-purpose cleaner. She wiped down the walls and door, as well as the top and bottom (the rotating glass tray), to ensure there were no spatters of cheese and sauce clinging to the insides of our kitchen pals. This isn't an easy task for Wilma, because she has to stretch in order to reach Luke and Nuke. Like we mentioned, our twin microwaves each have their perch, and Wilma is ... *hmm* ... How can we describe her state? Ah yes, she's "vertically challenged"!

(*Note: Yeah, in other words, she's short. —-Tom*)

(*Shush! —-Wilma*)

Wilma thought she'd thoroughly cleaned out Luke and Nuke, but when she reached up and felt around on their glass trays, she soon realized there was something still sticking to the glass. So she wiped the surface again, only harder this time. And yet, she could still feel something gritty. Something that felt "fuzzy" like rough cardboard. Wilma was understandably perplexed, so she fetched a stool in order to climb up and get a better look inside the mysterious workings of Luke and Nuke. (*Instead of standing on her tippy toes.*) (*Will you stop?*) (*Hee-hee, okay.*)

Once she got on the stool, and gained a higher point of view, she discovered that some of the paper from the pizza cartons had stuck to the glass trays. Apparently, the paper packaging of the average frozen food carton tends to stick when microwaved. Too bad the pizza company didn't list that little fact in their cooking instructions. But that's not our point here. What's important—according to Luke and Nuke—is that initially Wilma couldn't see the problem from her "short-sighted" point of view. Furthermore, she was unable to address the problem until she gained a better, higher view of things. (And address it she did, with a soft scouring pad and even more determination.)

In life, just as in the kitchen, we often face problems which leave us perplexed and not knowing how to proceed. But that's usually because we approach life from a short-sighted viewpoint. We continue to view our circumstances from a natural and temporal perspective; so we're unable to see the higher working of things. Then we attempt to fix things in our own strength—*we get on our tippy-toes.* However, when dealing with a truly "sticky" situation, this approach never quite works. We need a step up in order to gain a better, more spiritual look at life.

If you're facing a challenge today, we encourage you, first, to get a "higher" perspective of what's going on. Seek God through prayer and Bible study, and ask Him to help you see people and the problems of life the way He sees them. Learn to adopt a divine perspective of life. Second, don't try to solve all your problems in your own strength, "stretching yourself on tippy-toes" until you pull an emotional muscle. Grab a "spiritual stool" and take a step up.

The Psalmist writes, in "A Song of Ascents" [ascent as in climbing]: "I lift up my eyes to the hills. From where does my help come? My help comes from the LORD, who made heaven and earth. He will not let your foot be moved; He who keeps you will not slumber. Behold, he who keeps Israel will neither slumber nor sleep." (Psalm 121:1-4 ESV)

Ask God for His help and guidance. Ask Him for a helping hand and a spiritual boost up. Whatever you're facing, you are Not alone. Your problems did not catch God off guard or take Him by surprise. Trust Him, He's got this. So ask yourself, "Why are you down in the dumps, dear soul? Why are you crying the blues? Fix my eyes on God—soon I'll be praising again. He puts a smile on my face. He's my God." (Psalm 42:11 MSG) In other words, stop focusing on the problem and focus instead on the problem-solver: the storm-stopper, the miracle-working God of the Impossible.

Sometimes our circumstances seem harsh, but the Bible states, "We know that all things work together for the good of those who love God...." (Romans 8:28 GW) Understanding this simple truth is another "step up" to gaining a heavenly perspective. It's also extremely helpful to remember that people are *not* problems. But like all of us, people only *have* problems.

View that aggravating neighbor or irritable coworker from God's divine perspective: through the eyes of His love. Love covers a multitude of sins. (1 Peter 4:8) Then count your blessings—*not* your troubles—with a genuine spirit of gratitude. Concentrate on the Most-High God, and not on all the things that get you down in the dumps. Get a higher, spiritually-minded perspective of life ... from a perch well above the kitchen counters—*er*, above the trials and tribulations that clutter our wonderful, sometimes crazy, world.

...As the heavens are higher than the earth,
so are my ways higher than your ways
and my thoughts than your thoughts.
—Isaiah 55:9 ESV

Meatloaf Blues

THERE'S A SCENE from an old sitcom, and it plays something like this: a teenage boy walks into the kitchen and asks his mom, "What's for dinner?" After she tells her son that she's lovingly made his favorite, meatloaf and mashed potatoes, the boy whines, "Aww, meatloaf? I just came from Jimmy's house and his dad's grilling steaks." Who's to be pitied more? The poor mom who's slaved over the hot stove trying to please her family—or her ungrateful son, who's got the meatloaf blues, a symptom of "the comparison bug"?

Unfortunately, we all periodically suffer from this illness. It's a common malady of the human race, but there's a cure. Just stop. The kid in the aforementioned sitcom ought to have been happy that his mom cooked his dinner to start with—let alone made his favorite—and we would all do well to stop comparing what we have with what someone else has. Life is more enjoyable when we're grateful for what God has provided us. And, personally, we *love* meatloaf, with mashed potatoes and mushroom gravy. Of course, we serve a pretty mean meatloaf at our house.

Still, we tend to get caught up in comparing, and when we do, we inevitably reach the same conclusion: there's always something better than what we have. The neighbors are having steak and we're stuck with meatloaf. Or, we're having meatloaf but the neighbors are having meatloaf with mushroom gravy. Yes, the dinner is always more delicious on the other side of the fence—or is that grass?

After God led His people out of bondage from Egypt, He daily provided them with a perfect food called *Manna*. Manna was "a flaky substance" that "tasted like honey wafers." (Exodus 16:14,31 NLT) The Israelites collected the manna each morning, and we can imagine it might have been a little like Kellogg's Frosted Flakes. To quote Tony the Tiger, "They're grr-reat!!"

But God's people started comparing, as we all tend to do, and suddenly they were *homesick* for the foods they ate when they were slaves. *Seriously?* Yeah, the "comparison bug" really is a sickness; and we'll never truly enjoy life if we're always "sick" about what we could have, but don't have. How can we enjoy a delicious cool glass of freshly squeezed orange juice if we start contemplating what else we *might* have had? Remember the TV commercial for vegetable juice? The guy suddenly stops sipping his OJ, slaps his forehead and cries, "Wow, I coulda had a V-8!" Don't fall prey to the comparison bug. Enjoy the moment. "This is the day [or food, or home, or opportunity] the LORD has made. We will rejoice and be glad in it." (Psalm 118:24 NLT)

Another symptom of the comparison bug manifests when we start comparing ourselves to others. Trust us on this one: no matter how beautiful or talented you are, how much money you make, or how big your home is, there will always be someone somewhere who's just a little prettier, more gifted, more prosperous, more whatever. So ... since these things are all relative to begin with, then why compare —and compete? Catch the comparison bug and you'll probably also come down with "inferiority fever" followed by "insecurity sickness"!

On the other hand, there will always be those who don't seem to measure up to you and your standards. Should you take what God has blessed you with as a reason for pride? If you do, then you're suffering from the vanity virus.

We mentioned we serve a mean meatloaf. We have a friend who started comparing her cooking skills to Wilma's; and she felt she came up short. As a result, she was reluctant to have us over for dinner. Sad and unnecessary. We all have different gifts and abilities, and there's no point in comparing. When we do, nothing good ever comes out of it; instead, we miss out on the joy of life. But our friend was mature enough to confess she was feeling a little inferior in the kitchen. We told her not to worry: we're not into comparing and competing. And we're grateful whether we're served pheasant under glass or a plain pizza. Then we reminded her just how talented she was in areas that remain a complete mystery to us.

Our friend relaxed, realized what's most important, and then had us over for a take-out pizza. And we're not sure why, but apparently her fellowship added a lot of extra flavor to the food, because it was one of the best pizzas we'd ever had. *Get the lesson here?*

Please don't catch the comparison bug. At first it just makes you sick, but later it can kill your joy. "I ask you not to think of yourselves more highly than you should. Instead, your thoughts should lead you to use good judgment based on what God has given each of you as believers." (Romans 12:3 GW)

Remember the symptoms: the meatloaf blues, inferiority fever, insecurity sickness or vanity virus. Nip them in the bud before you get a bad case of the comparison bug.

People Shouldn't Act Like Peas

HELLO THERE, MY FRIENDS! I'm Mr Freeze, Tom and Wilma's faithful upright freezer!

When they asked me to tell you readers about frozen foods I naturally jumped at the opportunity. Well, actually I just sort of continued to stand in the corner of the room I share with Blue, the SUV. (Which for some strange reason, Tom and Wilma refer to as the garage.) Anyway, the history of frozen foods is a subject that's near and dear to my heart. In fact, just thinking about it sends chills down my cooling coils.

Believe it or not, people have been preserving foods by freezing them for hundreds of years. Fishermen and trappers first started the trend by storing their fish and game in unheated buildings during the winter. They had learned, quite by accident, that freezing foods slows down and even halts the forces of nature—namely, the growth of bacteria which otherwise hastens spoilage. But the first large-scale commercial use of preserving foods by freezing was in 1899, when warehouses in Russia routinely shipped about 200,000 frozen chickens and geese to London each week, where specially devised cold-storage facilities kept the meat frozen until it went to local markets.

Later, during the 1920s, the inventor Clarence Birdseye, introduced U.S. shoppers to his hugely successful frozen peas which, when thawed, tasted as fresh as the day they were shelled from their pods. These peas were preserved through Birdseye's ingenious process of *flash freezing.* Quick-freezing reduced the formation of large ice crystals, which can damage the taste and texture of foods.

Although the company started by Birdseye continues to be an innovator in the production of frozen vegetables and complete meals, today there are numerous businesses offering what companies such as Swanson once called "TV dinners"; as well as frozen pizzas, pies, cakes and ice cream —*mmm,* just the sort of heartwarming comfort food I keep in my frosty compartments.

Further advancements in frozen foods came about out of necessity: during World War II, the U.S. Military researched better ways of freezing orange juice and dairy products for troops serving overseas; and in 1957, when then-First Lady Eleanor Roosevelt visited Russia, the U.S. government devised new ways of packaging frozen foods for her trip. Speaking of Russia, I've always wanted to vacation in Siberia. I understand that year-round the weather is quite lovely.

But enough about me and my passion for all things frozen. I want to share an interesting observation about people: some of them are frozen—*like Birdseye's peas.* Not literally, mind you. But remember that I said freezing stops the forces of nature? In a manner of speaking, it puts life on hold—and sometimes people want to do the same thing.

There's a character in Charles Dickens' classic, 1861 novel *Great Expectations* who did just that: Miss Havisham stopped all the clocks in her house and then shut herself away from the world after she experienced a devastating disappointment. She was to be married, on what should have been the happiest day of her life. Many elaborate preparations had been made, including a long dining table exquisitely set and groaning beneath an abundance of gourmet foods; and crowning the center of the table, a wedding cake fit for a king and his queen.

All of Miss Havisham's guests had arrived to join in the celebration, and together they waited with the bride-to-be

—uncomfortably, for what seemed an interminable time— for the groom to arrive. But he never did. So, the wedding guests silently returned to their homes, and Miss Havisham, whose heart was broken, whose dreams died that day, withdrew from the world. She cloistered herself in her darkened mansion, with all the wedding preparations left untouched, preserved as a burial shrine to her dead hopes. The clocks stopped ticking and she stopped "living"! Miss Havisham, for all intents and purposes, allowed herself to become mentally and spiritually "frozen in time"; trapped like an ancient relic in the ice of her own pain and grief; unable to move beyond the disappointments and bitter memories of a single moment.

Brrr, pretty dramatic, huh? But, just like Miss Havisham, there are people today who, because of past hurts, mistakes and disappointments, are "frozen" in their own emotional and spiritual growth, no longer moving forward in life—no longer even enjoying life.

Have you made bad mistakes? Have you been severely hurt, betrayed, or disappointed? At one time or another, we all have. An even more important question is, were you "flash frozen" in your moment of grief and despair, anguish and disillusionment? Symptoms of being frozen include frequently reliving a past hurt, harboring a grudge, being afraid to trust again, or refusing to start over. If any of this describes you, it's time to come in from the cold: take steps to forgive and forget; make a conscious decision to put the past behind you, and then start moving forward.

It always helps to get things off your chest and out into the open, so consider talking to a trusted friend or a spiritual leader. If necessary, seek out a professional counselor. But above all, ask the God of all comfort to heal your emotional wounds. (2 Corinthians 1:3) "He heals the brokenhearted and binds up their wounds." (Psalm 147:3 ESV)

There's room for only one Mister Freeze around here— and that's me. But I only keep *foods* frozen. I like people well-thawed. And unless you're a box of snow peas, you shouldn't allow anything to keep you frozen. Don't allow someone who wronged you in the past to continue to steal your present peace and joy, or your future growth and happiness. Stop acting like a pea. Break out of the ice. To quote the lyrics of a popular song from Disney's *Frozen*, if there's something bothering you, "Let it go!"

"Weeping may last through the night, but joy comes with the morning." (Psalm 30:5 NLT)

Supersize It!

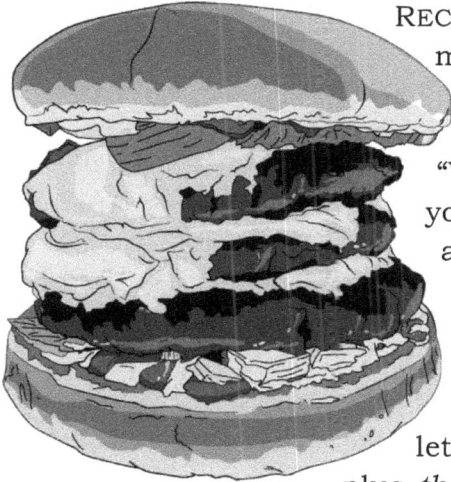

RECENTLY, WHEN WE ORDERED A meal at a fast food restaurant, the lady behind the service counter politely asked us, "Would you like to supersize your order?" We were slightly amused. The burgers were already huge: half a pound of charcoal-broiled ground beef on a thick sesame seed bun with double layers of lettuce, tomato, and pickle— plus *three* slices of cheese. It had a name like the "Sumo Wrestler Junior," which made us shudder to imagine the Sumo Senior! Oh, and it came with a bucket of fries and a gallon of soda.

Sure, we're exaggerating, but still, we're amazed at how the portion sizes served in American restaurants have grown over the years. We used to ask for a doggie bag so we could take home what we couldn't finish. Now when we ask, the waiter brings out a couple of big square Styrofoam containers, and we're able to pack up enough food for another big meal and a bedtime snack.

If you could time-travel back to the late 1950s or early 1960s, you'd probably be shocked by the serving sizes in a typical drive-in hamburger joint. A regular burger was one thin patty of beef with a dollop of mustard and ketchup; not the stacks of steer you get today. A pack of fries was about 2.5 ounces. Today a pack of fries weighs in at around 6.5 ounces. And the average-sized soda was 8 fluid ounces, not the 32-ounce "bladder-busters" served today.

Maybe all this supersizing was a response to the once meager portions served in finer restaurants: a medallion of meat the size of a political campaign button handed out by an underdog independent; three—count 'em—*three* tiny new potatoes artistically arranged next to a few slivers of carrots and zucchini on a plate the size of a saucer. Those were "healthy" portions ... for a hamster with a small appetite.

This is what's known as portion control, and we understand it's all the rage in expensive restaurants with fancy menus that don't list the prices. One portion-size fits all, from tiny *eats-like-a-bird* Barbara, all the way up to *gone-in-60-seconds-and-now-I'm-eyeing-YOUR-plate* Pete. Ah, the good old days of eat, drink, and still be hungry.

The Bible also speaks of portions: "'The Lord is my portion,' says my soul, 'therefore I will hope in Him.'" (Lamentations 3:24 ESV) But exactly what kind of portion is God providing His believers? Does anyone ever leave our Heavenly Father's table still hungry—and needing to supplement their portion with a snack?

No way. Those who come to God's table quickly realize, "Whom have I in heaven but You [God]? And there is nothing on earth I desire besides You. ...God is the strength of my heart and my portion forever." (Psalm 73:25-26 ESV)

In other words, the portion served by God doesn't leave us hungry for anything else.

God is not stingy. In fact, He's into supersizing His blessings: "[God] is able to do immeasurably more than all we ask or imagine according to His power that is at work within us." (Ephesians 3:20 NIV) And if that weren't enough, our Heavenly Father also serves *double* portions: "Instead of shame ... you will enjoy a double share of honor. You will possess a double portion of prosperity in your land, and everlasting joy will be yours." (Isaiah 61:7 NLT)

Have you endured hard times, or suffered through hurts and disappointments? Our Heavenly Father is also known as Jehovah El Gmolah, or the "God of recompense." (Jeremiah 51:56) The word recompense means: to reward, compensate, or provide restitution. So, in accordance with His divine nature, God has promised us that "...I will restore to you the years that the locust has eaten.... And ye shall eat in plenty, and be satisfied, and praise the name of the LORD your God, that hath dealt wondrously with you: and my people shall never be ashamed." (Joel 2:25-26 KJV)

We all know the story of Job, a prosperous man who lost everything. Well, God made sure Job's story didn't end there. "...The Lord restored his fortunes and gave him twice as much as he had before." (Job 42:10 NIV) Double what he had before?!?! Remember, Job had been a very rich man. Hence, doubling his original blessings was like ... super-sizing an already huge meal.

"The Lord blessed the latter days of Job more than his beginning." (Job 42:12 NASB) What encouraging words for those of us who put our faith in God, knowing that the best is yet to come. Double portions! Supersized blessings! (And no indigestion!)

Jesus Christ said, "I came that they may have life and have it abundantly." (John 10:10 ESV) Have you allowed God to supersize your life yet?

Cloudy, with a Chance of Meatballs

MEATBALLS! SWEDISH, ITALIAN, or sweet 'n' sour—we love them all. And there are so many wonderful ways we can use them. Spaghetti and meatballs, meatball subs, meatballs sliced and layered in lasagna, tiny meatballs on toothpicks as appetizers....

We have three favorite recipes. We make traditional Italian meatballs using ground beef, veal, breadcrumbs, grated parmesan and Romano cheese, tomato sauce and seasonings. These are great in a variety of Italian pasta dishes, but especially spaghetti and meatballs.

We've also made chicken meatballs by substituting shredded chicken and cheddar cheese. We like to serve these with rigatoni, instead of spaghetti. And we frequently make Swedish meatballs for get-togethers. Our Swedish meatballs are seasoned very differently, of course, and are served in a brown sauce made with sour cream and no cheese. These are to die for, especially when served atop a plate of egg noodles.

Although we've never tried these other recipes, we find it interesting that meatballs can be made from ground sausage, venison, or other meats, and seasoned in a variety of ways. What makes a meatball is not so much the ingredients as that beautiful round shape. One day we were making meatballs—lots of meatballs—for a gathering, when a friend dropped by unexpectedly. We invited her to join us in the kitchen, and talk to us while we worked.

As she watched, we'd scoop out a portion of the meat mixture, and gently but firmly shape each meatball by hand. She was amazed that we had it down to a science: but no real measuring; we'd just guesstimate the portions and roll them each into an almost perfect ball—quickly and efficiently—placing the nearly uniform meatballs on a large tray. We were like potters working with clay, molding, shaping, creating little culinary ornaments.

In a manner of speaking, each of us is a potential meatball in the making. No, not a "meatball" in the derogatory sense of "a foolish or stupid person." But God wants to shape and mold each of us for His purposes. Once we become the right "shape" spiritually, God is best able to use us to serve His Kingdom and the people around us. And like the great variety of meatball recipes we stated above, God is able to use whoever and whatever we are today, season us with the influence of His divine Holy Spirit, and then gently but firmly shape us into something beautiful.

Trouble is, many of us don't allow God to do the shaping. We refuse to be flexible, pliable.... Many of us are rigid in our thinking and our habits; and most of us are determined to "shape" our own destinies. In other words, many of us refuse to place ourselves, who and what we are at present, into the hands of the Master Chef, in order to allow Him to mold us.

God wanted His followers to understand this important truth, so He told His prophet Jeremiah to go to the potter's workshop. Once there, Jeremiah observed that often the vessel "...the potter was shaping from the clay was marred in his hands; so the potter formed it into another pot, shaping it as seemed best to him." (Jeremiah 18:4 NIV) Then God told His prophet, ask My people "...Can't I do with you as [the] potter does with clay? ...You are like the clay in the potter's hands." (Jeremiah 18:6 GW)

Are you allowing God to mold you? Are you soft, flexible, pliable, willing to place yourself into the hands of the Master? To be good clay (or ground beef), we must be teachable, willing to learn from God, the Bible, or anyone who shares a truth with us. To be flexible, we need to be receptive to new ideas (as long as they don't countermand God's sovereign Word). To be pliable, we need to be willing to surrender to God's will, and give up our "right to be right." (We can't expect to get everything our way.)

We may all start out as a pile of raw hamburger, with our prospects looking cloudy, but there's always a chance of meatballs—if we allow God to shape our lives.

The Nose Knows

DURING THE 1980s there was a cool commercial for a leading brand of plastic wrap. We say "cool" because it featured a Bengal tiger. Hey, ya gotta respect a tiger. Tigers outrank every other mammal. After all, just look at all their stripes. (That joke was a real stinker. Right?)

In the TV commercial, two thick, juicy steaks are completely covered in plastic wrap: one in the big-name brand, and one in their competitor's product. Both steaks are then tossed into a cage with a ferocious, starving (and quite handsome) tiger.

The big cat pays no attention to the meat covered in the advertiser's plastic wrap—because the tiger can't smell it. However, he devours the steak covered in cheap food wrap in record time, because he could smell the meat through the plastic. The advertiser's point was that their wrap didn't allow any air (and hence, aroma) to pass through, so it kept food fresher. As Mr. Spock would say, "Fascinating." But that's not the most interesting aspect of the commercial.

Taste and smell work together. Have you ever walked into someone's kitchen and smelled a cake baking. You probably weren't hungry until the aroma from the oven smacked you right in the kisser. And yet, after getting one whiff of cake, you start salivating like one of Pavlov's dogs for a thick slice of dessert. What happened? Well, the aroma gave you an appetite for what you were smelling.

Our sense of smell actually works together with our sense of taste. God in His wisdom gave us both senses, and here's why: people are like tigers; we usually won't try a new food unless it appeals to our sense of smell. Hey, the nose knows. Which is also why we usually smell food for freshness, well before committing ourselves to the first sip of milk or bite of cheese.

We can tell you that a certain food—one you've never tried before—is absolutely delicious. But if you can't smell that it's good, then you essentially have to take our word for it. We can even serve it to you on a tray with a fresh daisy beside it; but if there's no aroma to help trigger your appetite, there's a good chance you won't try it. On the other hand, if something smells delicious to you, then you'll probably go out of your way to ask us to share it with you.

Throw a steak on the grill. Once it starts to sizzle, and that smoky barbecue aroma fills the air, your neighbor will suddenly remember it's time to return the weed-eater he borrowed last month. He'll be leaning over the fence, hypnotized by the smell of the A1-Sauce,® and hoping he gets an invite. Of course, we've all been on both sides of the fence —not hungry until we encounter some intoxicating aroma.

So, where are we going with this? Well, faith and works go together the same way taste and smell do. Our faith in God, along with the joy and abundant life He brings when we trust in Him, are something we'd love to serve to our neighbors. One huge problem, though: they don't know just how good the things of God are. They've never tasted them before. Perhaps, they're not even "hungry" for the things of God. Although we can continually tell them just how "tasty" a believer's life is, unless there's a delicious aroma to entice them, to alert them to something delicious, there's a good chance they won't try it. Sad, but true.

That's where the aroma of our faith kicks in. Just as good food emits a wonderful fragrance, so too should our faith—and our lives as followers of Christ. The Bible states, "...We are the aroma of the Messiah ... the sweet smell of life leading to more life." (2 Corinthians 2:15-16 CJB) This pleasing aroma is emitted when we demonstrate what we believe in. When we love others, when we give, serve, and encourage those around us (in essence, when we're being hospitable[9]), the pleasing aroma of godliness attracts our neighbors just like the smell of the backyard grill. Whether we call it "good works" or "faith in action," demonstrating what we believe in will always make others hungry for what we can share.

"...Through us, [God] brings knowledge of Christ. Everywhere we go, people breathe in the exquisite fragrance. Because of Christ, we give off a sweet scent rising to God, which is recognized by those on the way of salvation—an aroma redolent with life." (2 Corinthians 2:15-17 MSG)

Jesus commanded us not to hide our light (the light of truth) under a basket, where no one can see it. In the same way, don't "store your beliefs under thick plastic food wrap." Instead, allow the world to smell the sweet aroma of Godliness—by living out what you believe. When you do, the aroma of your good works will help create a genuine appetite for the good things of God; and your friends, family and coworkers will come around asking, "That smells delicious! Can I please have a taste!"

---

[9] See page 197 for more on the Biblical concept of hospitality.

"Taste and see that the LORD is good! How blessed is the person who trusts in him!" (Psalm 34:8 NIV)

The Smell of Freash Bread

OUR FAITHFUL KEURIG COFFEEMAKER gets up before we do. His built-in timer awakens him a few minutes before our alarm goes off, so we arise each morning to the rich aroma of freshly brewed coffee. And seriously, it's much easier to roll out of bed and face the day when you're greeted by the promising fragrance of French roast.

The fragrance of foods plays a big role in our enjoyment of life and, specifically, working in the kitchen and preparing for holidays. Around Thanksgiving, we look forward to the wonderful bouquet of a pumpkin pie baking in the oven, of hot apple cider sprinkled with cinnamon, and a piece of seasoned redwood crackling in the fireplace. At Christmas we delight in the scent of apple strudel with vanilla sauce, and festive garlands made of fir cuttings and pine cones.

Smells can communicate powerful messages to the brain—sometimes of a subliminal nature. They can attract or repulse us; put us in a relaxed mood or make us feel anxious. They can make us hungry or cause us to lose our appetites; and they have the ability to conjure up vivid images of the past. In fact, many of our fondest memories are usually linked to the smells of childhood. That's why the aroma of fresh baked bread can transport you back to the home of a loving grandmother; and the perfume of freshly-mown grass can remind you of summer days long gone and family cookouts with ripe watermelon.

The Bible frequently references the sense of smell to illustrate some important truths. For instance, the Apostle Paul wrote, "Live a life filled with love, following the example of Christ. He LOVED us and offered Himself as a sacrifice for us, a pleasing aroma to God." (Ephesians 5:2 NLT) God's signature fragrance is love.

In the Old Testament, God's people would offer Him symbolic sacrifices. (See Exodus 29:18, 25 and Numbers 15:5) The "soothing aroma" of these offerings anticipated the ultimate sacrifice made by Jesus Christ on the cross, which paid—once and for ALL—the penalty for our sins. Therefore, "...We have been made holy through the sacrifice of the body of Jesus Christ once for all." (Hebrews 10:10 NIV)

Christ is often called the Bread of Life. (John 6:32-35, 48 and 51) The sacrifice of the Holy Bread of Life released the most intense "soothing aroma" of God's signature fragrance: LOVE!

"For God loved the world so much that he gave His one and only Son, so that everyone who believes in Him will not perish but have eternal life." (John 3:16 NLT) Love. It's the "essence" of our Heavenly Father, who He is, what He works in His divine wisdom, and Why He accomplishes it. Love is God's delicious and comforting aroma of the Bread of Life.

Can you smell the Love of God in your life? Today God is proclaiming to you, "I love you with an everlasting love. So I will continue to show you my kindness." (Jeremiah 31:3 GW) What a rich and wonderful aroma!

Knock Knock!

IN THIS SERVING OF WIT AND WISDOM—as communicated through the sights, sounds, and aromas of the average kitchen—we pay tribute to the Doors. No, not the Vietnam War-era rock group. We don't need Jim Morrison to "Light My Fire"! (When we do need a flame, we have our trustworthy gas range, Sparky, one of the many angels in our kitchen.) We mean the *doors*, thse swinging elements of hip architectural design, upon which great things hinge. (Get it? Hinge? Doors? Sorry.)

Doors help divide various areas, while still offering easy access. Doors can be used either to keep something out or to allow something in. Cool, right? "Ah," you wonder, "but what sort of wisdom can plain old doors teach us? And regarding the average kitchen, where exactly do they come into the picture?"

These multitalented swingers actually have a very special message for our readers. And we find them everywhere in the kitchen, doing their part to make our lives wonderful. The door on the microwave keeps us from getting nuked along with the popcorn. The door on the refrigerator keeps cold air in and hot air out; and the oven door does just the opposite. Big deal? Well, remove any of these doors and you'll quickly learn just how big.

There are cabinet doors, hiding the clutter of canned goods above the counter, and the boxes and bottles of cleaning products below. And in our own kitchen, we have this adorable little door on the front of our appliance garage. He rolls up whenever we need the services of those kitchen avengers, the mighty Thor (a powerful blender) and our "talking" toaster (able to brown four slices of bread in a single bound—*er*, push).

While we're gushing about doors, we'll point out that our kitchen at Woodhaven is surrounded by doors on every side. We all know that the kitchen is the heart of the home, the center of life-sustaining activity lovingly expressed through the meals flowing forth to the entire household. (Wow, that's poetic.)

At Woodhaven, however, our kitchen is literally at the heart of things. It's located in the middle of several other downstairs rooms: on one side are the foyer (separated by double doors) and the dining room (separated by swinging doors); on the opposite side are French doors opening onto a meager porch; at one end is a breezeway, again separated by a door, which leads to a powder room and the laundry; and finally, at the opposite is our library with a good solid door to keep out kitchen smells. Yes, our kitchen is a square—but all of our doors are swingers.

Having a library adjacent to the kitchen may seem odd, but both rooms are key hangouts at Woodhaven. One supplies food for the soul, the other food for thought. And when we're writing in the library, we like having easy access to our Fridgey—who holds the blessings of cold drinks, leftover pizza, and ice cream bars. But in order to get to the kitchen, the heart of our home, we need a door. And, unless we can pass through solid walls like Casper the Friendly Ghost, we need to *open* that door.

There's another kind of door we all have. We can't see it, but it works either to keep things out or to let things in. It's the door to the human heart—and its proper use hinges upon our own free will. Only we can open this door.

Jesus said, "I stand at the door and knock. If you hear my voice and open the door, I will come in, and we will share a meal together as friends." (Revelation 3:20 NLT) God wants to enter into the "kitchen" of your life: your heart. Have you given Him easy access by opening the invisible spiritual door? When you do, you'll enjoy the blessings of an intimate relationship with your Heavenly Father, as well as eternal life.

If you're still shut away from God, then please open the door and invite Him in. Don't try to figure out all the hows, whys, and wherefores of God, and don't put it off—or you'll probably forget. Besides, do you really want to leave the Creator of the Universe waiting at the door.

"For God loved the world so much that he gave his one and only Son, so that everyone who believes in him will not perish but have eternal life." (John 3:16 NLT) "...Everyone who calls on the name of the LORD will be saved." (Romans 10:13 NLT)

And once you've opened the door to Christ, please don't confine Him to just the "kitchen." Let Him have the full run of the house—every area of your life—and then He can help you clean out those messy "closets." Visit with God every day by spending quality quiet time with Him through prayer, worship, and the reading of His Holy Word. You'll get to know Him much better, and you will also grow spiritually.

Shh! Hear that? Someone's knocking at the door!

Close the Door!

IT'S TRUE. Our refrigerator helped teach us one of the cold facts of life.

Fridgey, as we fondly call him, is one of our most faithful kitchen angels. He's pretty talented, too. Fridgey keeps the romaine lettuce crisp in its compartment, protects the frozen fruit for our smoothies from thawing, and makes a big bucket of ice cubes— all while dispensing refreshing filtered water from his sparkling white door. And he loves it whenever we open that door, to gather the items needed to prepare a meal, or to just grab a snack, and in general, to take advantage of his tireless efforts to preserve our food. Yes, we can almost see him smile.

But does he brag? No way. Fridgey is one of those tall, strong, silent types that never gets upset or rattled, an even-tempered appliance that's content to quietly stand by, always ready to serve. You might say he's a very cool character.

But Fridgey does have his moments. He can get a bit testy if we leave his door open for too long. In fact, he'll actually *beep* his displeasure. We get it, of course. Leaving the refrigerator door open allows moisture to get in, and it causes Fridgey to have to work harder.

Which is why moms and dads have always admonished their kids—who have this tendency to stand for long minutes in front of an open refrigerator, seemingly spellbound by its culinary contents—*to shut the door!*

We confess: we're guilty of leaving Fridgey's door open. But it's usually because we're stocking or removing several items at once, or a large platter that takes two hands, and then we sort of forget to close the door. That is, until Fridgey reminds us. We still haven't learned to speak his language, but we get the gist of what he's saying. *Beep!* (Hey!) *Beep beep beep!* (Shut the door!) With all those beeps, we sometimes wonder if Fridgey's vocabulary might be laced with "colorful metaphors"!

Poor Fridgey is saying: "Do you want all the yummy stuff inside to go bad? Do you want all my efforts to protect what's inside to be for nothing? Do you want me to fail at what I was created to do?"

Finally, we sheepishly responded: Of course not, Fridgey! We appreciate all you do for us, and we are truly sorry. We promise to be more careful; and to close the door as soon as we get what we need. We didn't mean to upset you or keep you from fulfilling your purpose.

And we meant what we said. We also consciously worked to form the good habit of closing Fridgey's door. This is what's known as repentance: changing one's mind and changing one's destructive behavior; basically, turning around one's life. So, once again, things are going well in our kitchen. We're doing what's right, and Fridgey is back to quietly and contentedly serving. He's very forgiving, like all our kitchen angels.

By the way, Fridgey is not the only one who benefits and functions best when the door is closed. We humans also need to "close the door"! We should close the door to negativity (or stinking thinking): focusing on the bad instead of the good; constantly complaining instead of being grateful for the good things in life (which greatly outnumber the bad).

We need to close the door to anger, hatred, unforgiveness, gossip, and anything else that hinders and damages our relationships ... with God the Creator, and with our fellow travelers on this spinning world of ours. After all, relationships are *the* most important thing in life. Which is why Jesus, summarizing The Ten Commandments found in Exodus 20, said "'You shall not murder, you shall not commit adultery, you shall not steal, you shall not give false testimony; honor your father and mother,' and 'love your neighbor as yourself.'" (Matthew 19:18-19 NIV);[10] and also why the sacred practice of hospitality is greatly needed in our world today.[11]

We must close the door to prejudice and stereotyping. We should never label people and try to pigeonhole them, forming our opinions of others on the basis of external and superficial characteristics or practices —in order that, as Dr. Martin Luther King, Jr. stated in his famous "I have a dream" speech, "one day all people will live in a nation where they will not be judged by the color of their skin but by the content of their character." (August 28, 1963)

And we must close the door to bigotry, racism, and antisemitism (which once again is on the rise), always

---

[10] See "Boiling it Down," on page 178.
[11] Read a special preview of *The Heart of an Angel*, on page 195.

mindful that we are all created in the image of God. (Genesis 1:26-27) Indeed, we are all members of a single race—the *human* race.

In the same way that Fridgey has a built-in mechanism that beeps to let us know we need to close the door, to prevent his contents from spoiling, the Lord tells us to close the door to unwholesome and destructive mindsets and behaviors, to keep what's inside *us* (our heart and mind) from being spoiled. And although the Lord doesn't beep, He nevertheless communicates to us through a built-in mechanism, for God created each of us with a *conscience*, which allows His Holy Spirit to "speak" to us regarding what's right and wrong.

"When the Spirit of truth comes, He will guide you into all the truth...." (John 16:13 ESV) "...And you will know the truth, and the truth will set you free." (John 8:32 NIV) Free, that is, from anything that can hinder your relationship with God and with other people.

Friends, like our faithful Fridgey, our Heavenly Father is crying out, "Close the door"—to all the things in life that are harmful to both you and your fellow man, including all the destructive tendencies we've discussed here. And we learn *how* to close the door to such hurtful things by following the Word of God: "All Scripture is God-breathed and is useful for teaching, rebuking, correcting and training in righteousness, so that the servant of God a may be thoroughly equipped for every good work." (2 Timothy 3:16-17 NIV)

To *really* close the door to our darker side (our fallen nature) and appeal to our "better angels" (our changed hearts), we need only follow and apply God's principles, as laid out in His "operator's manual": the Bible. One such principle is known as the Golden Rule. Matthew

7:12 defines it: "So in everything, do to others what you would have them do to you, for this sums up the Law and the Prophets." (NIV)

Let the Bible be your guide, and listen for God's occasional "beeps"—He's saying "Close the door!"

Can You Say Sorbet?

SHHH! We're about to point out the differences between sherbert, sherbet and sorbet. But first we need you to chill. (Sad attempt at humor, right?)

Sherbert is far easier to explain than to type. Our spell-checker continues to flag the word as a mistake. It's not, though. Sherbert is to sherbet what catsup is to ketchup—simply an alternate spelling that's used informally. The spelling of sherbert matches up with the way most people pronounce the word. You'll never see the word at the grocery store. But you'll hear it from shoppers looking for a frozen dessert called *sherbet.*

Sherbet is made of frozen fruit juices, sugar and a small amount of milk or cream. The quantity of dairy products in sherbet is what distinguishes the treat from other types of frozen

desserts. Sherbets contain 1% to 2% milkfat. A similar product but with a milkfat content between 2% and 10% is termed a "frozen dairy dessert"—which seems mysteriously vague unless you know that the word ice cream is reserved for frozen treats with a milkfat content of 10% or higher. As Yoda might say, "Now revealed to you, the mysteries of the universe are. Herh herh herh."

If you remove all the dairy from sherbet, you have yet another frozen dessert, which is called sorbet. Some people pronounce the word "sore bet"—which sounds like a tip on a horse race that failed to pay off—but hey, when in France, remember to *say*, sor-*bay* (sôr'bā). (All of which rhymes, by the *way*.) And should you find yourself in one of those fine French restaurants, you will likely be served a sorbet between the courses of your meal. But it's okay to eat "dessert" between the stuffed-mushroom appetizer and the escargot. In fact, the head chef will be glad you did, because it will allow you to better taste the next dish he's painstakingly prepared.

A sorbet is a soft icy mixture made from pureed fruit or concentrated fruit juices. A mint or lemon sorbet is often used to "cleanse the palate" or wash the tastebuds, of any overpowering spices or flavors in foods. A sorbet gets rid of the taste of the last thing a person ate, enabling him or her to better enjoy the delicious, and occasionally subtle, spices and flavorings in the next food served. Sounds snooty? Yeah, but it works. And sometimes we need to get rid of the taste of one thing before we can fully appreciate the next thing.

Are you ready for the next thing? In life—sooner or later—we all go through tough times. We encounter loss and failure, disappointment and heartache. Many of us have to endure the pettiness of narrow-minded people: jealousy, hatred, and prejudice regarding age, sex, ethnicity, economics, education and experience. These negative experiences can leave "a bad taste in our mouths"! We might even start viewing life through our bitterness, and adopt a sour perspective of people, things, the Bible, and even God. So it's important we cleanse our spiritual palates.

The Word of God is a "spiritual sorbet" for the bad taste that lingers after a bad experience. It can refresh our perspective of life. However, we actually need yet another spiritual sorbet to allow us to fully "taste" the sweetness of God's Holy Word; to fully appreciate (and understand) it. Before we partake of our spiritual food we need to cleanse our perspective with prayer. Prayer helps us to receive and "digest" everything our Heavenly Father has seasoned His Word with. It opens up our understanding to the fullness of God's plans and desires for our lives.

Here's a prayer sorbet to prepare us for God's spiritual food: pray, "Teach me, Lord, the meaning of Your statutes, and I will always keep them. Help me understand Your instruction, and I will obey it and follow it with all my heart." (Psalm 119:33-34 HCS)

When it comes to God's daily bread, there's logos or a general application and understanding. But there's also *rhema*, in which a specific scripture really hits home. It leaps off the page, and you know it's a special word God wants to speak to you at that particular moment; a word for a particular situation or problem you're dealing with; a promise that will sustain you throughout the day, and carry you through the storm. Thank goodness, you could fully savor it, because you prayed away the bitterness, sour attitude and nasty taste from any bad experiences. And then you prayed for understanding.

At least, we hope that's what happened. Or did you allow some recent course in your life to flavor your understanding of a key verse? After all, God's Bread of Life—without the spiritual sorbet of prayer—can taste like moldy cheese. So, before you crack open your Bible, first cleanse your "palate" with prayer. Ask the Lord to open up your understanding, to guide you, and to help you apply His Word.

Can you say "sorbet"? We thought you could.

The Truth about Triangles

TRIANGLES CAN OFTEN SPELL TROUBLE. Legend has it there's an area in the western part of the North Atlantic Ocean where numerous ships and planes have mysteriously disappeared. This loosely defined area has been called the Bermuda Triangle, or—The Devil's Triangle. Now, we're not exactly sold on the idea that of all the various shapes, the triangle is the most insidious; but its particular geometry has a history of vexing people.

Egypt's great pyramids may have been a place of rest for the Pharaohs of Old, but not for the slaves who labored to construct these imposing stone monuments. And what did the average "underpaid" laborer working on King Tut's tomb behold? The four triangular faces of the pyramid.

Sinister, right? And in school, when he wasn't throwing spitballs, the worst kid in band class got to play the ... triangle. Perhaps there's good reason the triangle belongs to a type of musical instruments labeled *idiophone*. (Funny? Hey, this is the kind of stuff that's just too crazy to be made up.)

And in life, love, and relationships, triangles always cause emotional pain, and usually end in disaster.

The shape of a triangle has 3 sides and 3 points. A triangle relationship involves 3 people and has 3 sides (to the story). In a marriage, an emotional triangle can lead to spiritual and/or physical adultery—requiring a fourth person to get involved, one with a law degree. Please don't go there. Adulterous triangles are hard to square with God and spouses. (Pun intended.)

If you're dating, then you know triangles can be just as aggravating outside a marriage. It's hard to have a meaningful relationship with a friend (or parent, or brother, or sister, or even a family pet) whose attentions and loyalties are divided. People are, after all, naturally selfish, self-centered and possessive. So, having a third-party present, especially one who's competing for attention (and even affection) can be aggravating.

Johnny Mathis recorded a popular song about the woes of a triangle in dating. "I seem to be the victim of a cruel jest," he crooned. "It dogs my footsteps with the girl I love the best. She's just the sweetest thing that I have ever known; But still we never get the chance to be alone. My car will meet her—And her mother comes too! It's a two-seater—Still her mother comes too!"

We don't believe Mathis was singling out moms, because he includes a verse about sulking at his club—only to have his girl friend's brother tag along. "There may be times when couples need a chaperone; But mothers ought to learn to leave a chap alone. I wish they'd have a heart and use their common sense; For three's a crowd, and more—it's triple the expense!"

There are situations, however, in which three is *not* a crowd, and the poor, teary-eyed triangle gets an opportunity to redeem his much-maligned geometry. The first is in the kitchen. (See? We may fly off on a tangent, but we always find our way back to the heart of the home.)

Designers and architects frequently express the need to arrange the cook top, the sink, and the refrigerator into a shape that ensures each is only a few steps from the others. The primary tasks involved in preparing a meal are carried out between these three kitchen angels, and reducing the distance between them reduces the time and energy spent cooking. The three workhorses of the kitchen should form a triangle; and according to designers, the imaginary lines between the sink, range, and refrigerator should be no more than nine feet.

This idea seems new, but it actually dates back to the 1940s. Efficiency experts dubbed it the "kitchen work triangle," correctly stating that food storage (from the refrigerator), preparation (at the sink) and cooking (on the stove or range) are easier and less tiring when these three elements are closely gathered in a triangular formation.

We've visited some homes with cavernous kitchens, in which the cook needed roller skates to get from the range to the sink to the fridge. The acoustics in these humongous kitchens are absolutely amazing—the beeping of the microwave produces a pleasing echo as the sound bounces from wall to distant wall —but preparing a meal in such a space can be exhausting. The kitchen work triangle creates an efficient and well-ordered arrangement that facilitates life in the heart of the home.

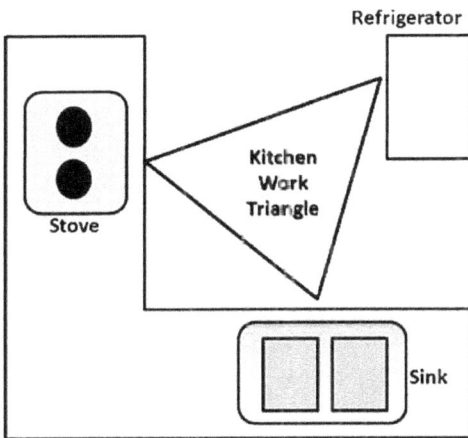

There's another triangle that's indispensable. One which creates an efficient and well-ordered arrangement, and facilitates the heart of life. It's called the spiritual triangle. In the endeavors of life, the triangle is formed between you, your pursuits (dreams, decisions, activities, job, hobbies, etc.) and GOD. In relationships, the triangle is formed between you, your spouse (or friend or family member, etc.) and GOD.

When you commit to being one of the parts of the spiritual triangle, your life will be well-ordered and your activities will seem less

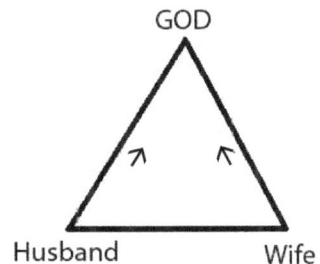

tiring. Your life will become more efficient, so to speak; spiritually efficient, because including God in your plans will facilitate all you do. But it's not enough to simply include God in your geometric pattern for living; like the kitchen work triangle, the spiritual triangle operates at peak efficiency when the three parts are close together.

Being closer to God, more deeply connected, helps maintain the primary tasks of the heart (life, love, and relationships). His infinite love, His wisdom, and His guidance all work together to ease the everyday struggles of life. Furthermore, in relationships, His presence strengthens the bonds between people, and keeps clean-ups to a minimum. When we have a good relationship with God, we're better equipped to handle relationships with others. God and other people, the two are closely tied together: "Jesus said, Love the Lord your God with all your passion and prayer and intelligence. This is the most important, the first on any list. But there is a second to set alongside it: Love others as well as you love yourself. These two commands are pegs; everything in God's Law ... hangs from them." (Matthew 22:37-40 MSG)

The third peg in the spiritual triangle can be *you*—if you're willing to surrender to God (by letting Him call all the shots), and draw closer to Him through worship, prayer, and Bible study. By the way, doing so is crucial to a successful marriage: take a look at the diagram of the relationship triangle again, and observe that as a husband and wife both move closer to God, they also move closer each together.

So, next time you're in the kitchen, look for the work triangle. Let it remind you of God's love for you, and His divine wisdom and power, which can abundantly facilitate all you do. God's spiritual triangle will always make life easier, and you can always trust Him to keep you anchored in your corner.

"Two people are better off than one, for they can help each other succeed. ...[But] three are even better, for a triple-braided cord is not easily broken." (Ecclesiastes 4:9, 12 NLT)

A Trail of Bread Crumbs

REMEMBER THE CLASSIC fairy tale about Hansel and Gretel? It was written by the Brothers Grimm in 1812, and tells the story of two children who were led into the woods by their wicked stepmother. (Stepmothers get tons of bad press in fairy tales.) The children are abandoned in the forest, and would be hopelessly lost ... except that, unbeknownst to their evil "guardian," these two resourceful kids had scattered a trail of breadcrumbs the entire length of the journey.

We will return to this exciting tale after a few brief words about breadcrumbs.

Before the advent of pre-packaged, commercially available breadcrumbs, cooks had to make their own. (No, they didn't collect the crumbs that fell into everybody's lap while eating cookies in front of the telly.) They baked their own bread, first of all, and once a loaf went stale, they'd grind the hardened bread into crumbs. Some people still make their own breadcrumbs today, but we imagine it's much easier now, as you can simply throw toasted chunks of bread into a food processor.

Years ago, companies such as Progresso began offering Italian-seasoned breadcrumbs for use in recipes for making meatballs or breading veal or eggplant parmigiana. They also distributed "traditional" or unseasoned breadcrumbs for making meatloaf, breading Southern fried chicken, and the like.

And now, back to Hansel and Gretel. We last left our hapless heroes leaving a trail of breadcrumbs behind themselves as they are led astray in the darkness of the woods. *Tsk, tsk.* Guess what? Essentially, we're all like Hansel and Gretel. Life is far from being a fairy tale, but as we journey through it, we leave behind us an unmistakable trail of crumbs, the bits and pieces of broken relationships, crushed dreams, and shattered lives.

Like Hansel and Gretel, many of us are often led astray —not by a wicked stepmother, but rather by the foolish decisions we make. We get entangled in unwholesome relationships, fall into destructive habits, and listen to wrong advice. Our mistakes in life often carry us deep into the woods. We find ourselves lost and alone in a dark forest of our own choosing. But whether or not it was our intention, we've left behind us all the broken pieces of our lives. It's a clear trail of disappointments and disillusionment, of sorrow and bitter tears; a distress signal only God can see and hear—and truly understand. You see, when He walked with us here on earth, our Lord was described as "...Despised and rejected—a man of sorrows, acquainted with deepest grief." (Isaiah 53:3 NLT)

In the fairy tale, Hansel and Gretel had to fend for themselves. And ultimately this brother and sister were forced to find their own way back home. Although they do eventually make it, they encounter along the way a horrible witch who tries to make a meal of the two kids. But even in this fairy tale God was there to help. Gretel, overcome by fear, prays a simple prayer: "Dear God, pray help us."

And—*warning: plot spoiler*—He did!

Our loving Heavenly Father follows our trail of breadcrumbs to find us, rescue us and bring us to His "home"; He restores both us and our relationship to Him. Paul writes, "...God showed His great love for us by sending Christ to die for us while we were still sinners." (Romans 5:8 NLT)

Even when we don't acknowledge Him as the Creator of the Universe, even when we neglect to include Him in our lives, even when we know what's right but do what's wrong —He nevertheless follows the trail we leave behind. He longs to rescue us from the dark woods.

Are you out of the woods yet? God is still searching for people lost in the forests of life: broken people with nothing to offer Him but the crumbs of their lives. "He heals the brokenhearted and bandages their wounds." (Psalm 147:3 NLT) Only God, the Master Chef, can gather our bread-crumbs and use them to create something truly delicious.

Good Gravy or Grave Glop?

COLONEL HARLAND SANDERS always said his original fried chicken was so delicious because it was prepared from a "secret recipe of 11 herbs and spices." Perhaps at one time the tasty batter-coating *did* contain 11 herbs and spices. Today, however, KFC (the company that now owns the Colonel's name and secrets) may need to check their math. There's a good chance the corporation has myth-calculated the number. In fact, after procuring a batch of the season-ing and having it analyzed, William Poundstone wrote in his 1983 book *Big Secrets*, the formula consists only of flour, salt, monosodium glutamate, and black pepper. (Hurray, at least pepper *is* a spice.)

We're not bashing KFC—we still like their chicken—but we do wish to point out a truth. "Stuff" has a way of changing, not always for the better, and often we don't even realize it. Or, to paraphrase an oft-used sentence, "What you think you see, is not necessarily what you get."

We trust that when Colonel Sanders began franchising his famous fried chicken, way back in the 1950s, he did use "11 herbs and spices" (ingredients he insisted "stand on everyone's kitchen shelf"). But times change, and apparently so does the truth—*or does it?*

Regardless how many are used, herbs and spices add flavor, aroma, color, texture and, often, nutrients to many recipes. [Time out. Do you know the difference between *herbs* and *spices*? *C'est simple!* Herbs are produced from the green leafy parts of certain plants. Spices are produced from parts of certain plants other than the leaves. Basil, made from leaves, is an herb. Ginger, from the root, is a spice.]

Sanders, who devised many of the recipes and cooking processes used at his outlets, once said his signature gravy was so delicious, "You'll want to throw away the chicken and eat the gravy." However, after the Colonel sold the food chain to a big corporation, the gravy formula quickly changed—without prior warning. Sanders, staying on as spokesperson for a time, compared the new gravy to wallpaper paste. He was known, whenever he popped in to inspect one of the restaurants, to throw the gravy against the wall, and a few choice words (or "colorful metaphors," as Star Trek's Mr. Spock once termed them) at the staff. Oh well. His name was on the product, after all; but he knew it was no longer the real deal.

Other things changed, too. For instance, Colonel Sanders always fried his chicken in pure vegetable oil, because he felt doing so yielded the best flavor. After purchasing the chain, KFC changed the cooking oil to save money. Soybean oil was substituted because it's cheaper, albeit more fattening; but the corporation wasn't exactly planning on publicizing their "fixes." Again, we're not necessarily

faulting KFC. To succeed companies always have to watch their bottomline. Still, it's nice to know when things change and exactly what you're getting.

In good faith, Colonel Sanders shared his recipes and sold the use of his name. He imagined that wherever the words *Kentucky Fried Chicken* were displayed, and whoever prepared his signature food, the same quality and ingredients were assured. Imagine his dismay when he visited various KFC restaurants, sampled the menu, researched the ingredients.... Isn't anything sacred? Perhaps not these days.

In life, things change—often subtly. Whether it's in relationships or institutions, products or services. Sometimes substitutions are made. Things may look the same, sound the same, and even be labeled the same. But, as Colonel Sanders learned the hard way, regardless of the name, "chicken and gravy" ain't always what you think; and the same can be said of everything, including misleading things you hear on the evening news and read on the internet, which people then innocently repost on social media. Face it, there's a lot of misinformation in the world today.

Even what's often touted as Spiritual or Biblical truth may actually be a misrepresentation of the Word of God or, worse, outright FALSE. An obvious example of this is the frequently repeated remark that "money is the root of all evil"? Sadly, this seemingly harmless misquoting of the Bible has done its fair share of damage. Money is a tool. With it you can build hospitals and save lives. As an evangelist once put it, "If money is truly the root of all evil, then the Devil would be delivering it to your doors by the truckloads." No, the *true* Bible verse states, "...The love of money is a root of all kinds of evil, for which some have strayed from the faith in their greediness, and pierced themselves through with many sorrows." (1 Timothy 6:10 NKJV)

There are countless other instances of spiritual error, in which people have purposely altered or entirely dismissed Biblical truth to support their own agendas. Many of these people misrepresent the teachings of Christ in order to justify a particular behavior or lifestyle that is contrary to God's Word.

The Apostle Paul warned, "...A time is coming when people will no longer listen to sound and wholesome teaching. They will follow their own desires and will look for teachers who will tell them whatever their itching ears want to hear. They will reject the truth and chase after myths. But you should keep a clear mind in every situation...." (2 Timothy 4:3-5 NLT)

So, regardless of how it's labeled, how it's packaged, where it's served—always trust but verify. Don't swallow everything you hear. Know exactly what you're "consuming." What seems to be the "Colonel's gravy" (truth) may actually be nothing more than some "concocted glop"! And that's a grave (serious) thing to contemplate.

Cinnamon Deceptions

REMEMBER THE DIFFERENCE between herbs and spices? Herbs come from the green, leafy parts of certain plants. Basil, oregano, and mint are herbs; and the 1960s folk-rock duo Simon and Garfunkel included a few others in one of their somber songs: "...Parsley, sage, rosemary and thyme." Of course, when we were kids we thought they were crooning about breakfast sausage and the Sands of Time.

Spices are derived from parts of the plant other than the green leafy bits. Cloves (flower buds), ginger (roots) and pepper (seed pods). And then there's ... *cinnamon*. Oh yes, how can we forget cinnamon. To mention that we love it would be an understatement. In French toast, how much cinnamon is enough? Answer: More!

Are there any songs that mention cinnamon? None we know. But the Bible signifies this aromatic and flavorful spice in several passages. It was included in God's recipe for holy anointing oil, when "...The Lord said to Moses, 'Take the finest spices: of liquid myrrh ... of sweet-smelling cinnamon ... and of aromatic cane ... and of olive oil...; and you shall make of these a sacred anointing oil....'" (Exodus 30:22-25 RSV)

Solomon wrote "I have perfumed my bed with myrrh, aloes and cinnamon." (Proverbs 7:17 NIV) Other references to cinnamon are found in Solomon's Song of Songs 4:14; and in Revelation 18:13. We like to think that the Creator of the Universe loved cinnamon as much as we do.

But what's so special about this particular spice? In addition to tasting and smelling absolutely divine, cinnamon is loaded with fiber and antioxidants, and it contains a unique compound called *cinnamaldehyde*. These components make cinnamon conducive to good health. Indeed, the spice is known to produce 7 health benefits. (*Seven*—hey, that's God's favorite number.) Cinnamon: (1) can lower bad cholesterol or LDL; (2) can help treat Type 2 diabetes; (3) has antifungal, antibacterial, and antiviral properties; (4) can reduce the symptoms of Alzheimer's and Parkinson's; (5) has anti-carcinogenic properties; (6) has anti-inflammatory properties; (7) and can help manage polycystic ovarian syndrome, or PCOS.

And did we mention it's delicious in French toast? No wonder cinnamon was once valued almost as highly as gold, and was considered a gift fit for a king ... or a god. Cool, right? But times change. So does "stuff"! Not all is as it seems. And not all cinnamon is really cinnamon.

The English word cinnamon can be traced back to the Hebrew *qinnamon*, a spice imported to Egypt from India. This is known scientifically as *Cinnamomum verum*. You may recognize the Latin adjective *verum*, from which we derive such words as *truth* and *verify,* as in "Trust ... but verify."

"True Cinnamon" is produced from the inner bark of an evergreen tree that's native to Sri Lanka. *True* cinnamon was rare and expensive during Biblical Times. It was delicious, aromatic, and had many health benefits. It's what God requested be mixed into His Holy anointing oil.

But there's another spice currently marketed under the name "cinnamon." It's less expensive and more readily available. It's produced from the bark of trees originating in China and now cultivated throughout Asia. Spice manufacturers call it *Cassia,* to distinguish it from the real deal. Cassia *looks* like cinnamon and *tastes* like cinnamon—but contains none of the cinnamaldehyde or antioxidants that promote true health.

To the contrary, Cassia contains massive concentrations of a blood-thinning compound called coumarin. Consuming large amounts of this ersatz cinnamon as a health supplement, or maniacally tossing it into French toast batter, can lead to kidney and liver damage.

Who knew that something traditionally prized and sought after, something beneficial and even Biblical, could be replaced with something toxic? But again, the same can be said of many things, including the evening "news" and a lot of stuff that gets posted on the internet. So we can no longer accept things at face value.

Nor can we always go by the "label." This also applies to people—who often aren't what they seem or proclaim to be. How many of us have learned this truth the hard way? How many of us have trusted someone only to find out too late that he or she had a hidden (and self-centered) agenda? Even the Bible warns us against "wolves in sheep's clothing." (Matthew 7:15)

Let's be clear on this point: Not everyone who calls themselves a Christian is truly a follower of Christ. Again,

labels are convenient and ultimately can be deceiving. Even Satan sports a misleading label. Many of us (thanks to pop culture) imagine him as this red dude with horns and a pitch fork, but the Bible states, "...Satan disguises himself as an angel of light." (2 Corinthians 11:14 NLT) Why? Because he is "a liar—indeed, the inventor of the lie!" (John 8:44 Complete Jewish Bible)

In regards to all things, ask the Lord to help you distinguish the truth from the lie. Ask Him to grant you the ability to discern truth from error. And always do a little homework. Ask yourself, "Does *this* or *that* line up with the Bible, the infallible Word of God?"

Is it nourishing and beneficial? Or is it something spiritually toxic in disguise. Above all, is it *true*?

Don't swallow life's "cinnamon deceptions." Jesus said, "Take heed that no one deceives you." (John 24:4 NKJV) The Lord also said, "Not all who sound religious are really godly people." (Matthew 7:21 TLB) "The way to identify a tree or a person is by the kind of fruit produced." (Matthew 7:20 TLB)

Grape Expectations

WHAT'S A GRAPE TOPIC that's ripe for discussion? *Um*, grapes!

Grapes seem to pop up everywhere. They're in jams, jellies, and juices. They're made into wines, vinegar, and grape seed oil. They can be eaten raw, fresh from the vine, or dried into raisins. And there are several kinds of raisins, too. Although all dried grapes can be classed as raisins, currants are produced by specifically drying *Black Corinth* grapes. And Sultanas are made from white or red grapes.

Grapes are actually a type of berry; and despite there being many different varieties, all grapes are the fruit of the deciduous (leaf-shedding) vines of the botanical genus *Vitis*. No need to remember this word, there's no test. Seventy-two million tons of these berries are grown worldwide annually. Most of this fruit is used to produce wine—7.2 trillion gallons of it each year. *Hic!*

Grapes grow in clusters of 15 to 300, and are frequently distinguished by their colors: crimson, black, dark blue, yellow, green, orange, and pink. And for some reason green grapes are often marketed as "white" grapes. That's okay, but if you ever see something that looks like a grape but actually *is* white, you'll probably be better off not eating it.

Grapes and vineyards were prominent in Israel during Biblical times, and still are today. Because of their abundance, God uses them to teach His people several spiritual principles. For instance, all God's people share a few qualities with grapes. Yes, like these berries, we come in all colors, but the comparison doesn't end there. Grapes grow in clusters, and their dense groupings remind us that, again like the fruit, we were never created as independent beings. To the contrary, God designed humans to be interdependent.

People thrive in clusters. We are relational beings, who draw strength from the fellowship of others. In fact, when we're isolated and alone for long periods, we tend to grow loony. That's why God stated, "It is not good for man to be alone...." (Genesis 2:18)

Although this verse specifically refers to marriage, the first institution created by God, it also illustrates our Heavenly Father's intention that His people form mutually beneficial relationships—not only relationships with others, but also a relationship with Him. God didn't create us just to have something to do; He created us to have fellowship with Him. This is why the "greatest commandment" is to "Love God" ... closely followed by "Love your Neighbor"!

(Matthew 22:37-40) Oh, and by "neighbor" God means everyone.

Clusters of grapes grow in vineyards ... with other clusters; and people, in addition to being a part of a family unit, congregation, club, company or other association, are social beings designed to be members of a larger community. We call that community the human race.

In order to grow properly, grapes need a little help. The vines need a stronger, supporting structure upon which to grow. Without a trellis, or similar framework, the vines will trail through the mud and their fruit will rot. Similarly, we all need a little help from time to time—the support of a friend (or even a stranger). The Apostle Paul wrote, "Bear one another's burdens, and so fulfill the Law of Christ." (Galatians 6:2 NLT)

We have yet another support mechanism in God: "...The eyes of the Lord move to and fro throughout the earth that He may strongly support those whose heart is completely His." (2 Chronicles 16:9 NASB) God supports His faithful believers because He doesn't want us "growing in the dirt" like an unsupported vine, weighed down by grapes rotting in the mud.

Instead, God lifts us up so that we can flourish and become all He intended us to be. After all, we are created in God's own image (Genesis 1:26), for good works. You might say that, for each and everyone of us, God has Grape Expectations.

God Is Grape!

OUR FASCINATION WITH GRAPES continues, as these "berry" special angels in the kitchen "speak" to us. What's the latest gossip? Wine grapes, cultivated especially for wine-making, have thicker skins and are sweeter than table grapes. According to the grapevine, table grapes, like some people we know, aren't nearly as sweet and have rather thin skins. (Okay, we should behave now.)

Grapes were first cultivated in the Middle East about 8,000 years ago. The climate and soil conditions, particularly in regions of Israel, are ideal for growing grapes. In fact, the Holy Land has been called "The Land of the Grapes"!

When the Hebrews left Egypt and eventually returned to Canaan—the land of milk and honey the Lord first promised to the Patriarch Abraham, and which is now Modern Israel—God's people encountered enormous clusters of grapes. (Numbers 13:23) They reported that a single berry was the size of a plum. Imagine how impressive the fruit must have seemed to the Hebrews: in Egypt, grapes were the size of raisins; in Canaan, they could barely lift a cluster of the plump fruit.

Grapes quickly became the chief agricultural product of the region. The fruit is used to create a multitude of products: wine, raisins, and grape seed extract being just a few. Grape juice is also boiled down to the consistency of molasses to create a "honey" called *debash* (which may be the honey God spoke of in Genesis 43:11). Even the leaves are used in Mediterranean cuisine. Here in America, stuffed grape leaves can be purchased in cans at most food markets, and we sometimes serve them as appetizers.

As we previously discussed, grapes and grapevines were a large part of life in the Middle East, so God frequently used them as visual aids to teach important spiritual lessons. In the greatest of these lessons, in which He explains "How to lead a victorious life," God actually compares Himself to a grapevine. Jesus said, "I am the vine, you are the branches; he who abides in Me and I in him, he bears much fruit, for apart from Me you can do nothing." (John 15:5 NASB)

When God states "I am the vine," He is reminding us that He is the Creator and the Provider of every good thing. He's our Deliverer, our Healer, our Shepherd, our Peace, our Comfort in times of trouble, and the God who provides everything we need. And He tells us we are to be like the branches used in the vineyards, to lift the grapevines from the ground. In other words, we are to "lift Him up"!

If we could take a walk through a vineyard during the time of Christ, we'd see the branches of small trees being used the way gardeners use trellises today: the thick woody grape vines wrap around the branches of the trees, until it's hard to tell where the tree stops and the vine begins; or what belongs to the vine and what's part of the tree. This inseparable tangle of wood is a beautiful illustration of how we can become a part of God. As His "branches," we become His extended arms—and we grow to resemble Him in deeds and character. After all, we are created in His own image.

God then declares that if we "abide" in Him, we'll lead fruitful lives. The word abide means: to dwell and to rest; to remain, stay, or continue permanently in the same state or condition; to be firm and unmovable. God wants us to dwell with Him, to rest in His strong arms, and above all to stay connected to Him. We do this by fellowshipping with Him through prayer and Bible study. The Apostle Paul wrote, "Pray without ceasing" (1 Thessalonians 5:17 ESV). That sounds impractical and perhaps even impossible, but it's neither. It simply means to stay in constant communication with God, conscious that He's always there, submitting all one's thoughts and deeds to Him.

That's not to say we shouldn't daily set apart special quality time to spend with God, during which time He receives our undivided attention: in prayer, worship and scripture reading. Our attitude should be like that of King David, who wrote "O God, thou art my God; early will I seek thee: my soul thirsteth for thee...." (Psalm 63:1 KJV) We must keep God as our first priority—our first love (Revelations 2:4) —always giving Him the first fruits of each day.

Abiding in God also means being humbly and wholly dependent upon Him. Our own efforts are generally pretty pathetic anyway. But God declares that if we remain with Him, confidently relying on His strength and abilities, we will bear "much fruit"! How? Remember the illustration of the branch wrapped in grape vines? The vines are bearing grapes the size of plums, but since we can no longer determine where the branch ends and the vine begins, it looks like the branch is heavy with delicious fruit.

The fruit we bear through God comes in the form of good character, kind deeds, answered prayers, and the fulfillment of our greatest hopes and dreams; because God is able to "do infinitely more than all we can ask or imagine, according to the power that is working among us—to Him be glory." (Ephesians 3:20 ISV) In other words, we get the grapes, God gets the glory.

It's a sweet arrangement, because left to our own devices, and with all our human frailties, we "can do nothing" of lasting, eternal value. And yet, when we abide in God, we "can do all things through Christ who strengthens [us]." (Philippians 4:13) So, how do we look wrapped in God's loving vines? We look absolutely *grape!*

New Wine

HERE'S A JUICY BIT of culinary history that begins in 1861, when Charles K. Landis purchased 30,000 acres of agricultural land in New Jersey with the intention of creating an alcohol-free utopian society for himself and like-minded families who were willing to help farm the countryside and construct his "temperance town." Landis eventually named the town Vineland, because after discovering the soil and climate were ideal for growing grapes, the entrepreneur started selling 20-acre parcels to numerous Italian grape growers ... who quickly arrived and started growing grapes ... to use in the production of wine ... a fermented drink ... containing alcohol ... in a temperance town. See, fact is always stranger than fiction.

Vineland ultimately became famous for the grape adventures of Thomas Welch, a Wesleyan Methodist minister who lived a very full and colorful life. He was ordained at the age of 19 and, because the Methodists were staunchly opposed to slavery in America, Welch became active in the Underground Railroad transporting escaped slaves from the South into Canada.

Welch preached the Gospel until his voice played out—literally—and then went to medical school in New York. After becoming a doctor, and later specializing in dentistry, he moved to Vineland and set up a practice. Vineland was home to a large Methodist community, and Methodists were as staunchly opposed to the sale and consumption of alcohol as they were to slavery. However, since wine is served during communion services, this posed an interesting problem for the church.

Prior to the arrival of Welch, the church substituted grape juice, made by adding water to a juice concentrate, for wine. But in 1869, the good doctor invented a method of pasteurizing grape juice to stop the fermentation process. He then formed a company to manufacture *Dr. Welch's Unfermented Wine*, and persuaded local congregations to use his non-alcoholic "wine" in their communion services. So, next time you see a jar of Welch's grape jelly, or a bottle of the company's grape drink, remember that behind their label there's a history involving quite a colorful fellow.

And the next time you think about wine, consider this: The Bible does not prohibit the drinking of wine. Now, before we go any further, please allow us to state several things in our defense: first, we understand that people tend to be divided over the issue of alcohol: the consumption of alcoholic beverages can be habit-forming, leading to over-indulgence and drunkenness; and in many such cases, alcohol has destroyed careers, torn families apart, and claimed countless lives. Alcohol has earned a horrible and well-deserved reputation for being a catalyst for evil. So, if you're teetotalers, just as we ourselves are, then we applaud you. But the fact remains, alcohol was present in the wine consumed throughout the Bible.

Wine—*fermented* wine—was frequently enjoyed during what Gentiles refer to as *Jewish* holidays, which actually are *The Feasts of the Lord.* (Leviticus 23:2–4) Furthermore, Jesus Christ (Yeshua) chose to perform His first miracle at a wedding feast in Cana by turning water into wine. In doing so, Yeshua answered the anxious social concerns of His mother Mary, by saving His hosts from an embarrassing situation: running out of wine during a celebration—a definite no-no in a culture that viewed wine, celebrations, and hospitality as integral parts of life.

Wine was so prevalent in Biblical times, that Jesus used the subject of wine to illustrate several spiritual lessons. For instance, He stated, in Matthew 9:17, that new wine (symbolic of the Holy Spirit and salvation by grace through Christ) should never be stored in an old wineskin (symbolic of an inflexible, legalistic, usually hypocritical mindset that refused to accept the teachings and saving work of the Savior)—because the old wineskins would burst. Why? Because gases are released during the fermentation process that produces alcoholic wine; but new wineskins were "stretchy" enough to expand like a balloon. An old wineskin had lost its elasticity, and could no longer expand; instead, it would burst from the pressure of the fermentation gases produced by new wine.

So we have this significant scientific fact of life, along with several Biblical references, as proof that the wine being discussed in the Word of God is of an alcoholic nature—and not just grape juice. Alas, as every wino knows, too much of the "grape" leads to a dissolute life. Proverbs 20:1 states "Wine is a mocker, strong drink a brawler, and whoever is intoxicated by it is not wise." (NASB) Anyone who's had a little too much to drink can probably attest to this truth: alcohol lowers inhibitions, diminishes good judgement, and loosens the tongue. An overindulgence in strong drink can cause a person to lose control. When you're "under the influence," it's the alcohol that's calling the shots.

The Apostle Paul commands us not to overindulge in anything—or to lose "self-control," which is one of the fruits of the Spirit we're to cultivate. He writes, "...Don't get drunk with wine, which leads to reckless actions, but be filled by the Spirit." (Ephesians 5:18 Holman) Sound words.

Remember that Christ compared the Spirit of God to "new wine"? That's because the abundant life God grants each believer can be "intoxicating"—as long as we're abiding in Him. (John 15:5) It's the only "wine" we really need. It's impossible to overindulge in it, but even when we do, we don't have to deal with early-morning hangovers, or worry about the stupid things we did the night before. We don't lose control, but we do stay tuned in to God and ready for every good work. (Titus 3:1) See "God is Grape!"

In moderation, wine is okay. Alcoholic abuse is not; nor is letting strong drink control our lives. God set us free; let's stay that way.

Strong Wine

OUR HOME IN New Kent, Virginia, is within a short drive of two wineries. When out-of-state guests visit us, we like to take them to tour one of these companies nursing a process that's about 8,000 years old. As we previously stated, we're not wine connoisseurs. Nor do we imbibe alcoholic beverages of any type. But we do cook with it. And we find both the history and the process of winemaking an extremely interesting subject. Case in point: *GOD* created winemaking.

Okay, wait! Take a deep breath and try to relax. When God designed the grape, He impregnated the skins with a microorganism known as yeast. This microorganism occurs naturally on every single grape that ever grew on a vine—and it's the key ingredient needed to jumpstart the fermentation process, which produces wine from plain juice. So, if you crush grapes and leave the juice to its own devices, sooner or later the fruit sugars will ferment to alcohol. Hence, it was inevitable that God's people discovered a process that God in His wisdom engineered.

Grapes are an excellent source of antioxidants, and regular consumption of the fruit may yield several potential health benefits, such as the prevention of cancer, heart disease, and high blood pressure. But *wine* made from grapes seems to intensify these health benefits, and its alcohol content has a medicinal affect. In fact, the Apostle Paul instructed his protege Timothy to "Stop drinking only water, and use a little wine because of your stomach and frequent illnesses." (1 Timothy 5:23 NIV) No doubt the stress of shepherding a sometimes-contrary congregation was beginning to take a toll on Timothy in the form of an upset stomach, and a little wine can be soothing. Note, however, the key phrase "a little"!

As with several other wonderful things created by God, many people have abused alcohol and reaped the destructive effects of doing so; but God actually intended wine to be a comfort. Psalm 104:14-15 declares, "You make wine to cheer human hearts, olive oil to make faces shine, and bread to strengthen human hearts." (GW) The fermented drink was consumed during all of "The Feasts of the Lord" (Leviticus 23:1-2) which most people now refer to as specifically Jewish holidays. And Jesus made it the object of His first public miracle when He turned water into wine at a wedding feast.

Wine is furthermore linked to joy in a dozen Bible verses, such as, "[God's people will] cry out with joy... over the Lord's goodness, over the grain, the new wine, the fresh oil...." (Jeremiah 31:12 ISV); and "Fill my heart with joy when their grain and new wine abound...." (Psalm 4:7 NIV) The word *joy* is defined as a sense of well-being, gladness, or exhilaration of spirits—despite one's circumstances. It's the inner conviction that everything is going to turn out for the best, even in the midst of adversity. Joy is listed among the fruit of the Spirit, in Galatians 5:22; and it's cultivated by abiding in God (John 15:5).

Joy is one of the main themes of Philippians. In expounding on the theme, Dr. David Jeremiah writes in his book *Turning Toward Joy*, "The reason for Paul's joy was his relationship with Christ! ...We will observe the testing of that joy in the crucible of Roman imprisonment. If Paul's relationship to his Master could bring joy under those conditions, then surely we who also love the Savior can learn to rejoice in our difficult times as well."

Extended periods of sorrow, and a gloom-and-doom attitude can make you sick! On the other hand, "A joyful heart is good medicine." (Proverbs 17:22 NASB) So no matter what happens, no matter what someone says, it's far better to stay filled with the spirit of joy than to munch on sour grapes! Sour grapes will do nothing but pucker up your mouth, but maintaining your joy will actually empower you!

The Prophet Nehemiah stated, "Don't be dejected and sad, for the joy of the Lord is your strength." (Nehemiah 8:10 NLT) The prophet wrote this to his people during some truly tough times. But he was admonishing all of us that joy and strength are connected: they flow from the same divine wellspring.

Charles Swindoll states in his book *Laugh Again!* (also based on Philippians): "I know of no greater need today than the need for joy.... When that kind of joy comes aboard our ship of life, it brings good things with it—like enthusiasm for life, determination to hang in there, and a strong desire to be an encouragement to others.... There is nothing better than a joyful attitude when we face the challenges life throws at us."

Joy is like strong wine. But how do you keep your joy, and hence, your strength in the midst of a fallen and often negative world? First, you make a conscious decision to be

joyful, because joy, like love, is a choice—not a feeling. That's why Paul wrote, while sitting in a dirty prison cell, "Rejoice in the Lord always, and again I say rejoice." (Philippians 4:4)

Train your mind to focus on the positive, because you *are* what you think. (Proverbs 23:7) Continually count your blessings. Focus on God's love and acceptance, and be glad to be alive.

Don't get stuck in yesterday's disappointments. Each day is a new beginning with new opportunities. Declare each new morning, "This the day the Lord has made. Let us rejoice and be glad in it." (Psalm 118:24 Holman)

Stay in God's presence, because "...In [His] presence there is fullness of joy." (Psalm 16:11 ESV) How do we stay in God's presence? As we previously stated, by abiding in Him. Remember, Christ said, "I am the vine, you are the branches. Whoever abides in Me ... bears much fruit...." (John 15:5 ESV) We abide in Christ by staying closely connected to God, the source of our strength, through prayer and daily Bible study. Give God a little quality time each day, and let Him guide you in all things; and in return, He'll give you the strength to overcome life's challenges, both big and small.

No matter what comes your way, you'll lead a fruitful life characterized by contagious joy. Declare to God, "The Lord is the strength of my life!" (Psalm 27:1 KJB) Do it *now,* and say it out loud!

<blockquote>
...Let your face smile on us, LORD.
You have given me greater joy than those
who have abundant harvests ... and new wine.
—Psalm 4:6–7 NLT
</blockquote>

How to Avoid Brain Freeze

BRAIN FREEZE is that painful sensation you get—that feels like your head is about to explode—when you drink something really cold really fast. When it hits, all you can do is stop what you're doing and wait for it to pass. *We* know— we suffer almost daily, when we slurp our delicious fruit smoothies too quickly.

But there's another kind of brain freeze, which makes you feel like your head is about to explode; and it can stop you dead in your tracks; *frozen* in life, love, and the pursuit of all your hopes, dreams, and every creative thought— *struck by a glacier of loss, disappointment, and despair!* Brr!

Too much rejection too soon can do it. So can mistakes, dead ends, closed doors, missed opportunities, setbacks, weaknesses and failures.

The solution to avoiding brain freeze is to change one's perspective on life, problems, and failures; and to foster a *can-do* attitude. We need to look at our adversities as the perfect environment for personal growth; at setbacks as opportunities for comebacks; at our limitations as possible strengths; at our problems as invitations for innovation; and at a closed door as a sign to simply try a different door. And we need to learn to think outside the box. After all, necessity is the mother of invention.

Here's an example of someone who avoided brain freeze by following this advice, a savvy businessman who was definitely thinking outside the box (*above, beneath, and far beyond* an unexpected situation that would have frozen less enthusiastic people dead in their tracks).

His story begins at the 1904 World's Fair, held in St. Louis, Missouri, where an ice cream vendor suffered an acute attack of brain freeze when he suddenly realized he was unprepared to meet the demand for his frozen treats. Although there was a steady stream of customers who wanted his product, the hapless vendor was nevertheless about to pack up and go home—all because he had run out of the small paper containers he used to serve the ice cream.

Enter *Doumar the Undaunted*. Actually, our hero's name was just Doumar; *Abraham* Doumar, a sixteen-year-old immigrant from Damascus, Syria, who at the time was working as a traveling salesman. Doumar had been mingling with the crowd at the World's Fair, in an attempt to sell novelty paperweights, and he needed to take a break. He decided some ice cream would really hit the spot, but the first vendor he approached was "Mr. Brain Freeze" (he who hath run out of serving containers).

Doumar took a quick look around, and noticed a pastry cart nearby, where a man was selling Belgian waffles topped with a dollop of whipped cream. So he walked over and purchased one served plain. As Doumar returned to the ice-cream vendor, he gently rolled the soft, warm waffle into a cone. Then he asked Mr. Brain Freeze to fill the cone with a scoop of ice cream.

Voila! The ice cream cone was born.

Doumar also suggested the two vendors join forces, and soon these men found themselves swamped with requests for warm waffles with ice cream. Other vendors working the fair quickly copied the innovation—there were around fifty ice cream stands and over a dozen waffle carts in the park that day—and hence, several different vendors wanted to take the credit for inventing the waffle cone. Regardless, the treat caught on in a big way, and by 1924 Americans were consuming an estimated 245 million ice cream cones per year.

Doumar never bothered to patent his idea, but he did design the first machine especially built to bake cones. It was a four-iron waffle machine Doumar used three years later in Virginia, where, during the Jamestown Exhibition of 1907, he and his brother sold 23,000 cones in a single day.

Afterwards, Doumar designed a semi-automated, 36-iron waffle machine capable of turning out twenty cones per minute, and in 1934 he opened Doumar's Drive-In in Norfolk, Virginia. The restaurant is still open today, and still serving fresh waffle cones baked on Abe's original 1905 four-iron machine.

Now, don't think for a minute that Doumar didn't suffer through his own share of adversity. He had to weather the destructive forces of a hurricane, endure a few economic slumps, as well as the ever-changing dining habits of a more suburbanized world. Through it all, however, Doumar avoided brain freeze by thinking warm, friendly, "we shall overcome" thoughts.

The Apostle Paul similarly overcame tremendous adversity in the form of persecution, beatings, and a stoning so severe that his friends left him for dead. Paul also endured cold, hunger, and loneliness. He was shipwrecked and afterwards survived a venomous snakebite—at a time when there was no antidote.[12] But the much put-upon apostle who took the Gospel to the gentiles never suffered from brain freeze. Even while chained in a cold, damp, and dark cell in a rat-infested Roman prison, Paul wrote this warm proclamation: "I have strength for all things in Christ Who empowers me [I am ready for anything and equal to anything through Him Who infuses inner strength into me;

---

[12] Paul's travails are recorded in 2 Corinthians 4:8–18; 11:16–33; and Acts 27 through 28.

I am self-sufficient in Christ's sufficiency]." (Philippians 4:13 AMPC)

In other words, "Whatever I have, wherever I am, I can make it through anything in the One who makes me who I am." (Philippians 4:13 MSG)

This is a truth that can thaw the onslaught of painful brain freeze. *Remember it. Confess it. Believe it.* And refuse to be boxed in by your circumstances, limitations, or any adversity.

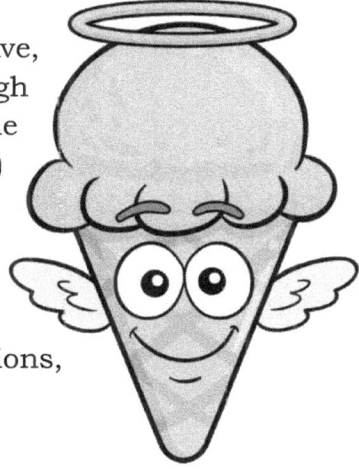

Chilly Challenges, Slushy Situations

DAIRY QUEEN SERVES a cold concoction guaranteed to create an addiction. It's called a Mocha MooLatté, an icy blend of strong coffee, intense chocolate, and fat-saturated cream. NASA would be wise to jettison orange-flavored Tang in favor of this slushy drink. Having future astronauts consume a Mocha MooLatté right before liftoff could save taxpayers tons of money in rocket fuel. In fact, our astronauts might even be able to reach Mars without a spaceship.

When we bought our first Mocha MooLattés, the lady behind the counter at DQ warned us, *"You'll be sooorry!"*

Really? How come?

"Because," she laughed, "you'll be back tomorrow for another one. And the next day and the next."

Visions of begging on a littered street corner suddenly filled our heads. We imagined ourselves pleading with passersby for spare change, all so we could buy just one more Mocha MooLatté—*Oh please!*

But the pusher at DQ—excuse us, the nice lady at DQ—was wrong. We had no intention of returning the next day. After we drank our slushy drinks, we got back in line immediately. Even she was surprised. Combining all that sugar, chocolate, and caffeine can definitely create an addictive rush, but the real danger in consuming this rich, delicious concoction ... this refreshing, invigorating ... incredible, absolutely divine drink —*gasp, we need help!*—is the dreaded side-effect that comes from careless and wanton consumption.

Ugh! BrAiN fReEZe!

Brain freeze is that sensation you get— that feels like your head is about to explode —when you drink something really cold really fast. However, as previously discussed, there's another kind of brain freeze, which makes you feel like your head is about to explode. It can freeze you dead in your tracks while in life, love, the pursuit of your dreams and goals. It's caused by the iciness of loss, disappointment, and despair; too many rejections, dead-ends, closed doors, missed opportunities, setbacks, weaknesses and failures.

As we previously stated, the solution to brain freeze is to change one's perspective on life, problems and failures; and to foster a *can-do* attitude. We need to look at our adversities as the perfect environment for personal growth; at setbacks as opportunities for comebacks; our problems as invitations for innovation; and a closed door as a sign to simply keep on knocking. Remember, *necessity* is the mother of *invention.*

Have you been frosted over by life's frequent frustrations? Here's a heartwarming story to help thaw your mind: In the late-1950s, Omar Knedlik, a WWII veteran who owned and operated a dilapidated Dairy Queen in Kansas City, created

another iconic frozen drink by sheer accident. Knedlik's restaurant equipment was always breaking down at the most inopportune times; and after his soda fountain finally gave up the ghost, Knedlik was faced with one of those potentially brain-freezing problems.

With customers to serve, each expecting a cold soda to wash down the burger and fries, Knedlik had to improvise: he loaded his freezer with bottled pop, which created a new problem. Knedlik couldn't get the hang of knowing just when to take the sodas out, so usually the bottles of carbonated liquid were partially frozen. And yet, his customers seemed to like the slushiness of these icy soft drinks, and would typically ask Knedlik if they could have one of the "pops that were in a little bit longer."

Knedlik immediately realized his troubles were blessings in disguise. Using the air conditioning unit from an old car, he built a machine in the back room which mixed and partially froze flavored waters and carbon dioxide, to create a slushy, fizzy drink he called *Icee.*

Most of us know Icee by another name: *Slurpee.* In fact, if you're like us, you might imagine that Icee, with its polar bear mascot, is a copycat of the more famous drink sold by the 7-Eleven chain. Not so. Icee is the original, but when Knedlik licensed the product to the convenience store chain, he asked that the name be changed so as not to limit further marketing deals. Now that's what we call fully thawed thinking.

Life is fraught with chilly challenges and slushy situations, but as the Apostle Paul wrote, "...Thanks be unto God, who always causes us to triumph...." (2 Corinthians 2:14 KJV2000)

Out of adversity come change, growth, and innovation. Understand this and you'll start viewing any circumstance, any problem, any setback as a new opportunity. *Every* experience, good or bad, provides a new opportunity to seek God, to ask for His wisdom and direction—and to press onward. And if you're a writer or an artist in drama, music, or graphics, these experiences are just more material for your work. If you're an innovator, every new challenge is grist for the mill, because the Lord is able to turn every curse into a blessing. (Deuteronomy 23:5)

So, if you want to avoid brain freeze, sip your Slurpees slowly and keep this positive perspective. Train yourself *not* to allow your problems, weaknesses, failures, setbacks, disappointments, dead ends, closed doors, or rejection to freeze your personal growth or progress. Always remember that "God causes everything to work together for the good of those who love God...." (Romans 8:28 NLT)

Cultivate this positive, victorious mindset, as well as a *can-do* attitude, and you'll never have to worry about getting brain freeze.

That Sinking Feeling

SO FAR, WE'VE WRITTEN about our kitchen angels Luke and Nuke, the twin microwaves; Thor, the mighty blender; Comrade Keurig, the coffeemaker; Mac, the knife block; Fridgey, the refrigerator; Sparky, the gas range; Mister Freeze, the upright freezer (who lives in the garage with Blue the SUV); and our feisty little toaster who talks. This swinging crowd of kitchen companions is frequently entertained by the musical broadcasts of Orson, from his perch on the country china hutch. Although we haven't discussed him previously, Orson is our handsome antique cathedral-style radio. And by the way, we're typing this on Hal, our ocassionally temperamental desktop computer.

We've also written about pots and pans, boxes and bags, weird cookbooks and funky foods. And that, dear friends, is pretty much the whole gang. Only we can't shake that sinking feeling that we've forgotten someone very important; that in our haste we've overlooked something vital to the smooth functioning of the kitchen. Oh, wait a minute. Hear that noise? It's the indignant gurglings of ... the sink. Okay, okay, that's Señorita Sink, thank you very much. And she's tired of being overlooked and underestimated.

Have you ever stopped to think just how important the kitchen sink truly is? It's the source of water in the kitchen, and without it, you can't maintain a continuous free flow of that water. After all, as the water flows out of the faucet, it also has to have a place to flow *to*—unless you want your socks getting wet.

The sink is a handy place to prepare fruits and veggies for salads and stews. It's also the place where we gather our dirty dishes—and the place where we wash them. Were we to suddenly lose our sink, we'd sorely miss it. We'd be losing an important member of our kitchen family, one which facilitates the roles of all the other appliances and gadgets. And yet, most people never even think about the sink. It's practically invisible, in fact: underestimated, devalued, neglected and overlooked.

When you visit the kitchen of a new homeowner, the host will excitedly show off the glistening new range, demonstrate the ice maker on the sparkling new refrigerator, and emphasize the spaciousness of the custom cabinets. But how often does he or she take you to the sink and gush about its wonders? When people walk into a home appliance showroom, they tend to gravitate to the section where the latest model washers, dryers, ranges and refrigerators are displayed. Does anyone ever head straight to the plumbing section—because they can hardly wait to check out the latest in new sink designs?

In society, we have an organization that's just as vital as the kitchen sink, and just as undervalued and overlooked.

It's the Church! Or, if you prefer, the Body of Christ; the local faith community; any place where believers assemble —a sink by any other name is just as neglected.

Your local church, like the sink, is a source of water, the water of the Word; and it facilitates the continuous free flow of the Word in our society. It's a place where spiritual food is prepared. It's a place where dirty dishes (soiled vessels for God) can congregate—and be washed. But we tend to overlook its importance and underestimate its influence in the proper functioning of our communities and ... even our government. And many of us totally neglect it. We don't drag our friends and family to it, while gushing about its many wonders. Nor do we consider its presence particularly important when we're shopping for a new home. It's often just an invisible afterthought in our towns and cities.

But were we to suddenly lose the church, and its Godly influence in society, we'd sorely miss it. Trust us, things just wouldn't be the same. So, ask yourself, do you have that sinking feeling you're neglecting something important? We hope it's not your neighborhood church.

Please, find a local faith community, attend regularly, and become engaged in serving. Support it, and pray for its hard-working spiritual leaders. "And let us not neglect our meeting together, as some people do, but encourage one another, especially now that the day of His return is drawing near." (Hebrews 10:25 NLT)

146

A Pleasing Aroma

AS PREVIOUSLY DISCUSSED, people are drawn to pleasing aromas. The smell of fresh bread baking in the oven will draw friends and family to your kitchen like bees to honey. And know what? There's one very pleasing fragrance that attracts our Heavenly Father. It's the irresistible aroma of *Praise!*

When we thank God and exalt Him in our words and music, we are in a sense offering up a sacrifice to Him: "the sacrifice of praise." (Psalm 50:23; Jeremiah 33:11; Hebrews 13:15) Sacrifices made in Old Testament times gave off a fragrance that God described as "the pleasing aroma of your offering." (Leviticus 26:31) As such an offering, our praise smells absolutely delicious to our Lord; and it draws Him near to us, the source of the "pleasing aroma"!

Psalm 22:3 teaches us that God "inhabits" or "dwells amid" the praises of His people. When we honor God with our songs of praise and worship, He quickly joins the festivities.

Having God close by is definitely a good thing. Besides, it's only right that we honor the One who blessed us not only with life, but also with *eternal* life.

"Praise the Lord! How good to sing praises to our God! How delightful and how fitting!" (Psalm 147:1 NLT)

But exactly how often should we praise the Lord?

"I will praise the Lord at all times [in every situation]. I will constantly speak His praises." (Psalm 34:1 NLT)

Now, please note: we're not asking you to praise God *for* rough times. We're asking you to praise God *during* rough times. King David, the Psalmist, went through some pretty bad situations, but he wrote, "I will praise You seven times a day because all your regulations are just." (Psalm 119:164 NLT)

What should we praise God for?

"...With my whole heart, I will praise His holy name. Let all that I am praise the Lord; may I never forget the good things He does for Me. He forgives all my sins and heals all my diseases. He redeems me from death and ... fills my life with good things." (Psalm 103:1-5 NLT)

Where should we praise God?

Wherever we are: at home and in school; on the job and at play—and *not* just in our local house of worship. The definitive answer, however, is "in His presence"; and He's *everywhere*. "Let us come into His presence with thanksgiving; let us make a joyful noise to Him with songs of praise" (Psalm 95:2 ESV)

Under what conditions should we praise God? In what circumstances?

Only when things are going our way, right? *Wrong.* Again, when we praise God despite of our circumstances, despite adversity and heartache, we really *are* making a "sacrifice of praise"! God realizes this, and He finds the aroma of our offering that much sweeter.

"...Let us continually offer to God a sacrifice of praise; the fruit of lips that openly profess His name." (Hebrews 13:15 NIV)

Facing a challenge? Struggling through a bad situation? Or are you just hurting today? Praise God anyway. Through your pain and tears. Praise directed at God will take the focus off *you* and your *problems* and put it instead on *God, the problem solver*. He's the miracle worker, the God of all comfort, and He'll join you *wherever* you are.

Praise Him. God will stay close by your side and work on your behalf. He'll calm your fears and raise your spirits.

Too Many Cooks

REMEMBER THE OLD ADAGE "Too many cooks in the kitchen spoil the broth"? It describes a consequence of having "too many chiefs and not enough braves." We frequently hear both of these idioms, and we generally agree that in this world there are way too many people who want to call all the shots. Now don't get us wrong, leaders are a vital part of every company, community, organization, family, and faith congregation: they usually know what needs to be done and how to get it done—or who to delegate it to. At least, we hope they do. And in their capacity as leaders—and perhaps we should qualify our statement—as *good* leaders, they fulfill the all-important task of ensuring things are done correctly and with a minimum of chaos.

Without a designated leader to organize activities and coordinate duties, you'll have two or three people trying to perform the same task, while another job gets completely neglected. We write designated because sometimes we need to appoint a person—one person—to lead, not because of their age, charisma or even experience, but simply to put an end to disorder. Obviously, the best qualified people should lead, but what happens when you have two potential leaders with equal qualifications?

Getting back to the kitchen, two cooks, both waving a spoon like a baton, while preparing the same dish, can end up serving an unpalatable mess. Think about our opening phrase: two conscientious and well-meaning cooks micromanaging a broth simmering on the range is an invitation to disaster. Guaranteed, one of them has already sufficiently seasoned the bubbling mixture; and guaranteed, the other cook will inevitably add another pinch of salt, white pepper, garlic, or something it doesn't need. The resultant broth will be too salty, too hot, or give diners bad breath for weeks.

In the finest restaurants, there are several chefs on duty: a Head Chef, a Sous-Chef (second in command), a Pastry or Dessert Chef, as well as chefs specializing in fish, vegetables, sauces … and the list goes on. All these chefs are highly skilled. Many could no doubt lead if called upon. However, at any given time, only a single chef is planning the menu and coordinating the efforts of his or her staff. If you dine in one of these five-star restaurants, your meal will almost always arrive hot and without an unwarranted delay; and if you walk into the kitchen, you'll see all the chefs working smoothly and efficiently with no misunderstandings, no confusion, no duplicated efforts, and no spoiled broth. Which is for the best, considering these restaurant kitchens maintain an impressive assortment of knives.

Here's another example: one commercial airliner, two capable pilots; both pilots have equal experience and skills, and both can fly the plane. But only one is designated as the pilot. The other member of the cockpit team is just as important, but has taken the subordinate position of co-pilot. This is a good thing, too. It ensures the passengers actually reach their destination.

As we stated, every company, community, organization, family, and faith congregation needs a designated "Head Chef" to ensure that whatever's "cooking" turns out right and with a minimum of confusion. The head guy isn't better or more valuable than the "Sous-Chef"; it's just the best way to get things done. This is especially true in marriages, particularly in the area of finances. Show us a couple with equal jurisdiction over their budget and expenditures, and we'll show you accidentally overdrawn accounts and needlessly missed payments.

Show us a committee where two people are trying to call the shots, and we'll show you a decline in volunteers. The same goes for any "family" unit, be it a business, club, or faith community. But the point we're trying to make is this: it's okay to concentrate on what you do best, and then follow a good leader. Even Jesus Christ understood this, which is why He remained under the headship of God the Father, stating, "For I have come down from heaven not to do My will but to do the will of Him who sent me." (John 6:28 NIV) It was the expedient way to accomplish His mission on earth.

True, someone has to be in charge, but it can't always be you. Nor can we always have our own way in matters. So, maybe it's time you got out of the kitchen (unless you *are* the head cook). Stop lifting the lids on all the pots. Stop tasting the broth every five minutes. And stop thinking that in every situation you need to put in your two cents' worth of spices. Be content to be the co-pilot, or the Sous-Chef, or just part of a bigger team. That's how things get done—quickly, smoothly, and efficiently—without bruised egos and busted noses; without kitchen chaos and culinary conundrums.

For God is not the author of confusion, but of peace....
Let all things be done decently and in order.
—1 Corinthians 14:33, 40 KJV

Vinegar and Oil

DECADES AGO, writers described the United States as a great melting pot of peoples and cultures, blended together to form something extraordinary. Later, we all realized the U.S. is actually more like a big salad bowl: our diverse cultures and backgrounds come together—and mix well—but these things still retain their identity and individuality. Imagine crispy croutons, cherry tomatoes and baby spinach leaves: they taste great together, but you can still pick out a crouton, hold it up to the light and ... it's still a crouton.

The same can be said of our favorite salad dressing, too. We keep a cruet of vinegar and olive oil (plus some seasonings) on the kitchen counter, and it serves to remind us of an interesting truth about the followers of Christ. Jesus prayed to His Father in Heaven, "I'm not asking you to take [My followers] out of the world, but to keep them safe.... They do not belong to this world any more than I do." (John 17:15-16 NLT) Now, to a non-believer this sounds a little insane, but we believe it. We believe that those who have accepted Christ are now His people. This "fact" has nothing to do with circumstances or anything we can see. We take this on faith.

We also take from this Bible verse the idea that "we're *in* this world, but we're not *of* this world"—meaning that we take part in society, playing an active role in everything, including government, but our connection is tenuous; we've become different (in a good way) and we're to remain separate. In other words, like the diverse cultures in our American salad bowl, we're not to lose our identity in Christ.

We're like the olive oil in the cruet. A hardy shake and we mix right in with the vinegar, but we never blend to the point that we lose our identity. Leave the cruet on the table for about 15 seconds and you'll see the oil quickly separates from the vinegar. Within a minute you'll have two distinct layers of liquid. Now, the reason we represent the oil is a no-brainer: once we accept Christ as our Lord and Savior, God's Holy Spirit comes to dwell in us—and throughout the Bible the Holy Spirit is represented by olive oil.

And the vinegar isn't a total misrepresentation of the world: our society, its people and culture; and the prevailing philosophy. Life in this world gets a bit acidic at times, and hence, people often tend to have a sour attitude and outlook. Acidic and sour ... like vinegar. And guess what? We need to be a part of this. When we come together with non-believers, we can make an excellent "dressing" that contributes greatly to the "salad" of ideas and cultures. But it takes an active and constant "mixing" on our part. We need to work to periodically shake things up. If we don't, we'll just settle out. And then we'll be useless as a salad dressing.

Any non-believer reading this may be wondering, does the "oil" think it's better than the "vinegar"? Not at all. The oil is actually here for the vinegar; and there can be no delicious collaboration without the vinegar. Plus, God reminds us that our salvation and association with God is nothing to boast in: "For by Grace you have been saved through faith. ...It is the gift of God, not a result of works, so that no one may boast." (Ephesians 2:8-9 ESV)

Hello, Oil? Please remember, "...There but for the grace of God, go I." (A well-known quotation attributed to the Christian martyr John Bradford)

Hello, Vinegar? Do you mind if we work together to make this great salad taste even better?

Beneath the Crust

IT'S OBVIOUSLY A MATTER of personal taste and preference: we love a loaf of crusty French bread—crispy on the outside, soft on the inside—and *one* of us absolutely adores the end slices from a loaf of bread. The extra crusty end piece from a loaf is known as the "heel." (In this case, you are *not* what you eat.) But apparently, there are those among us who don't particularly care for the crust, the chewier part of a daily baked essential.

We may like our bread crust, but we can still sympathize with those who don't. We can also remember a time from childhood when we mostly ate around the crust, leaving a pathetic-looking brown ring of overcooked dough on our plates. Sometimes, however, we'd prevail upon our parents to neatly trim away the crust on our jelly sandwiches, creating a nearly perfect square of tender, strawberry- or grape-flavored goodness.

Spoiled? No doubt. But for most kids, downing the crust from a sandwich is almost as daunting as swallowing multi-vitamins the size of horse pills. And it's not just kids who like having the crust cut off their sandwiches. Many adults do too. Which is why several companies market "crust re-movers." (Sounds euphemistic for a mafia hitman.) Most of these gadgets look like big square cookie cutters, and come with names like "The De-Cruster" or "The Krustbuster."

Removing the crust from a sandwich results in an almost magical transformation. A cheese sandwich *with* the crust is a ... well, a sandwich; something suitable for a picnic in the park, or a snack while watching TV. Cut away the tough crust, though, and suddenly your cheese sandwich is respectable enough to mingle with the guests at a wedding reception or other dressy occasion. A sandwich with the crust removed is transformed into a ... *canopay*(?) ... uh, *canopy* ... *canopoly*.... Sigh. A fancy little finger food fit for VIPs.

Sara Lee must recognize this truth: the company began marketing their "Crustless Bread" in 2009. (So now, you can have your cake and eat it, too; which never really made sense to us, by the way, because who in the world buys a cake unless they intend to eat it?) Also, chefs continue to devise new recipes that call for the crust people are cutting off their *cana* ... their sandwiches. Our favorite recipe is for bread pudding, so feel free to mail us your excised crust.

All this crusty commentary is to make a point: some people want this dry, chewy exterior removed. It's not a matter of being finicky; it's simply a matter of preference.

God likes the crust removed, and no one in their right mind would question the Creator of the Universe concerning good taste. God makes sandwiches? Not that we know of, but He does make people. And then He trims away the crust.

In baking, the exterior of the dough comes in contact with more heat, and hence forms a thick crust that's dryer, harder and tougher. In life, people take the heat of failures and rejection, mistakes and disappointments, pain and grief. People generally form a thick crust of fear and mistrust, selfishness and self-sufficiency, and often just plain grumpy unsociability. This protective crust is spiritually dry —not to mention tough and hardened. It insulates people from the world at large. It can prevent us from ever reaching the soft hearts buried within.

Ever meet someone with a crusty personality? *Crusty* is synonymous with irritable, cantankerous, bad-tempered, grouchy, snappish, and downright ornery. Or, to sum up *crusty* in a single word: uncivil. God created humans as relational beings. We were designed to enjoy the company of others, and to benefit from a close personal relationship with our Creator. So, the last thing God wants is for us to be crusted over by bad habits and attitudes, or just plain stinking thinking.

God transforms us by trimming away the hard crust. As a result, we slowly change, both naturally and supernaturally, from being an ordinary sandwich filled with sin and error ... to an extraordinary canapé that's tender and easy for others to partake. (Haha. Yeah, we actually do know how to spell that fancy little word.)

Next time you sense that God is cutting away some of the more-crusty parts of your life, just relax and rejoice— because He's preparing you for an exclusive gathering in His Kingdom.

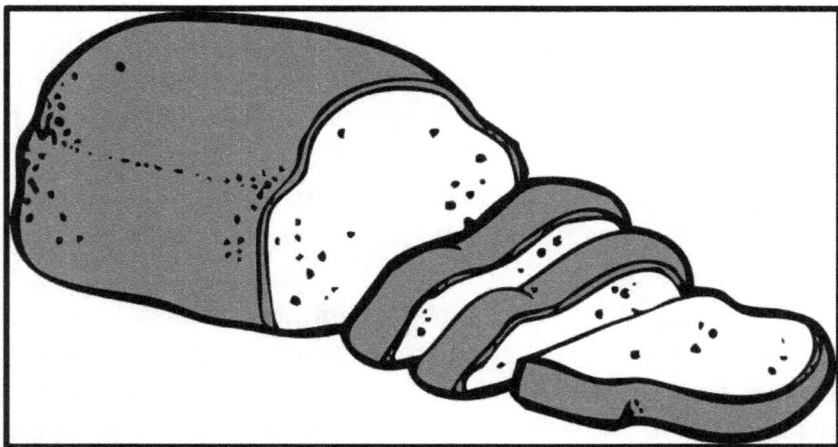

Today, if you hear His voice, do not harden your hearts ...
during the time of testing in the wilderness....
But encourage one another daily ... so that none of you
may be hardened by sin's deceitfulness.
—Hebrews 3:7-8, 11 NIV

Let's Talk Turkey

IN A LETTER TO HIS DAUGHTER, Benjamin Franklin wrote "...I wish the Bald Eagle had not been chosen the Representative of our Country." Apparently, the great inventor and one of the Founding Fathers of the United States fancied instead the wild turkey, a wily game bird that was plentiful throughout Colonial America, and which provided a rare feast for many of the families struggling to maintain a foothold in the New World.

Franklin wrote, "...The Turkey is ... a much more respectable Bird, and withal a true original Native of America... He is besides, though a little vain & silly, a Bird of Courage, and would not hesitate to attack a Grenadier of the British Guards who should presume to invade his Farm Yard with a red Coat on."

These are indeed fine and representative qualities for any National Bird, and no doubt, Franklin's intentions proceeded from a good heart. But imagine for a moment, our federal currency adorned with a sassy-looking turkey, beard and all; or this funky bird adorning our federal buildings. Hardly appropriate.

Let's talk turkey for a moment. It's the bird most associated with Thanksgiving Day dinner, and the traditional main course fancied by most people. That's what *we're* serving. And depending on who joins us at the table, there's also a chance we could be serving a ham or two.

During the preparations for our feast, our kitchen angels arise to their tasks with beeps, buzzes, and billows of silent steam. Sparky the gas range, while baking a turkey in his capacious oven, imagines he's like the great whale that swallowed up Jonah. We reassure Sparky, however, that our turkey will probably turn out far more tender than the hardened profit God sent to Nineveh.

Meanwhile, Luke and Nuke, the twin microwaves, frequently beep at the completion of their various chores: melting butter for various recipes or warming a few dishes we prepared the day before—because, yes, it pays to plan ahead and be prepared. And ocassionally Fridgey, our faithful refrigerator, whines at us because, after removing an armload of items from his spacious interior for the umpteenth time, we left his door standing wide open.

On the counter, Comrade Keurig surveys the scene while brewing cups of specialty coffees, which go great with all the seasonal pies we serve after the big meal. While under the counter, our grouchy Garbo (that would be our kitchen garbage pail) debates with our long-suffering Sinky (take a guess) what's the best strategy for mop-up operations once the big celebration is over.

As you can see, no one gets left out, because observing Thanksgiving is extremely important. Although many of us view the holiday as simply a time for friends and family to feast and fellowship—and some people have jokingly dubbed it "Turkey Day"—we should always remember the true meaning, significance and purpose of Thanksgiving, which we'll explore in the next tasty chapter, "The Secret Origins of Thanksgiving."

> Praise the LORD. Give thanks to the LORD,
> for He is good; His love endures forever.
> —Psalm 106:1 NIV

The Secret Origins of Thanksgiving

EACH YEAR, WE REMIND Mr. Turkey that Thanksgiving is *not* all about him! Which confuses this seasonal angel in the kitchen. "What do you mean?" he proudly gobbles. "I continually hear people refer to the fourth Thursday of every November as "Turkey Day"!

"Sad but true," we reply. And then we explain to Mr. Turkey that although he *does* play an important and even delicious part in the festivities, there's much more to the venerable holiday than just food.

"Are you sure?" he asks, eyeing us suspiciously. "I always assumed it was the one day out of the year when we get stuffed."

"Um, some of us *do* get stuffed ... on good food," we tell him with a touch of embarrassment. And then we share with this noble bird the true meaning of the holiday—the secret origins of Thanksgiving:

Thanksgiving originated as a celebration commemorating the autumn harvest. The first such celebration took place in 1621, in Plymouth, when the Pilgrims honored God with a three-day feast, thanking their Lord as their protector and the provider of the bountiful blessings they'd enjoyed all year. One of these blessings was the freedom to worship God without persecution. Another blessing was the peace and unity these colonists enjoyed in the New World: according to Edward Winslow, one of the attendees at this first Thanksgiving celebration, 53 grateful Pilgrims sat down to break bread with ninety Native Americans from the Wampanoag Tribe.

Elsewhere in America, New England colonists regularly celebrated "thanksgivings" or designated days of prayer thanking God for His continued blessings. But on October 3, 1789—when he made his *first* Thanksgiving Proclamation as the President of the United States—George Washington asked the country to observe the holiday *nationally*. And later, at the request of Congress, Washington ordered the first observance of Thanksgiving to take place on November 26, 1789.

Several decades later, in 1863, the 16th U.S. president, Abraham Lincoln, went one step further, by designating Thanksgiving as a federal holiday, a time of "Thanksgiving and Praise to our beneficent Father who dwelleth in the Heavens." Lincoln was correct, as he was in all things presidential, that we Americans owed an incalculable debt of gratitude to God for preserving the country through the turmoil and bloodshed of the War Between the States.

Together, these various celebrations and events formed the Thanksgiving traditions we now observe each year on the fourth Thursday in November. But do we always remember to express our gratitude to God? America is still standing, still free, still prosperous, still a land for which we should be especially thankful, a land founded upon Judeo-Christian principles; and yet, people today tend to celebrate the feast without acknowledging the Provider of the Feast.

One of the Hebrew names for the God of the Bible is *Jehovah Jireh*, which essentially translates "The Lord is my Provider." (See Genesis 22:14) It's wholly appropriate, because God's people understood that "Every good thing given and every perfect gift is from above; it comes down from the Father of lights [the Creator and Sustainer of the heavens]...." (James 1:17 ESV)

"And this same God who takes care of [us] will supply all your needs from his glorious riches, which have been given to us in Christ Jesus." (Philippians 4:19 ESV) Will you remember to thank the Great Provider and Sustainer during your Thanksgiving Day festivities?

Now, we fully understand that most people do not view Thanksgiving as a primarily religious holiday. Nevertheless, it is traditionally recognized as a day to give thanks, and to whom do we owe the most thanks if not the Creator of the Universe? In fact, the concept of giving thanks to God is woven into the fabric of Judaism and Christianity. Throughout the Bible there are countless scriptures on giving thanks, such as this one: "In everything give thanks; for this is God's will for you...." (1 Thessalonians 5:18 NASB)

Furthermore, God would wholeheartedly approve of Thanksgiving. We should daily count our blessings and thank God for His Love and care, but setting aside a special day to do so as a nation demonstrates the magnitude of our gratefulness to God for keeping our country and our families together and prosperous. In fact, God said, "You shalt feast in all the good things which the Lord thy God hath given thee and thy house, thou ... and the stranger that is with thee." (Deuteronomy 26:11 Douay-Rheims) *Hm,* sounds like a party—with God as the guest of honor.

So, when you sit down with friends and family today, before you carve the turkey, before you pass the sweet potatoes, remember to thank the Provider of your feast. And instead of muttering a quick and haphazard word of "Grace," tell God in your own words, and with sincerity, how much you appreciate His safekeeping and provisions. Later, after the meal, before you plop down in the recliner to watch the big game (or a movie classic), take time with your loved ones, to reflect on all the blessings you've reaped throughout the year. Thank the Lord for each one, and praise Him for His faithfulness. He delights in our praises, and He longs to hear our words of gratitude.

"It is good to give thanks to the LORD, and to sing praise to Your name, Most High." (Psalm 92:1 ISV)

And now that we've enlightened our feathered friend, he has a new message to relate: he wants everyone who sees a turkey to remember the secret origins of Thanksgiving. Indeed, this ocassional angel in the kitchen wants to remind us all to thank God, who not only supplies the food we eat, but also daily loads us with benefits and blessings. (Psalm 68:19)

What's Cookin' at Christmas?

PILLSBURY ONCE HAD AN AD SLOGAN declaring, "Nothing says lovin' like something from the oven." And we all know that "the way to a man's heart is through his stomach." Expressing love through food is an American tradition.

We've often written that the kitchen is the heart of the home. Just as our physical hearts pump the blood that sustains our bodies, our kitchens sustain our families, both nutritionally and emotionally, with a steady flow of home-cooked meals. Even if you take your meals away from home, somebody's kitchen is keeping you alive, whether it's at a restaurant, college cafeteria, or the company lunchroom that prepares those frozen dinners we all eat in a pinch. So, if you love food, ya gotta love the kitchen, too. It's where our meals are cooked, and the place where we most often enjoy them. It's also a great starting point for expressing love and hospitality.

While she was still with us, we'd often visit Tom's Granma—especially around holidays. How does that old Christmastime song go? "Over the river and through the woods to grandmother's house we go...." You know the rest. Except for the part about the horse and sleigh, the song pretty much described the long trip to her house: three hours of tree-lined interstate and the occasional billboard hawking fudge, fireworks and delicious pecan pies.

Gran-ma's home was small. The rooms were distinguished by old furnishings and outdated decor. Whenever we visited we always ended up in her kitchen; it's where she overfed us, and where we sat for hours, stuffed, happy, and chatting across the table. Gran-ma's table was set with mix-matched dishes, paper napkins, and oddly-placed silverware, all atop a tablecloth that really didn't go with anything. Her meals were simple fare, the Southern food Tom had grown up with, but ... *Ooh! How delicious!* Being a Northerner, Wilma was thrilled by the awesome taste and crispiness of Gran-ma's fried pork chops.

"It's just her usual hearty fare," Tom would say nonchalantly. "She breads the chops with crushed, seasoned, cornflakes."

Her "usual fare," the meal she had prepared with no fuss and no pretension, tasted absolutely gourmet. It was simply divine! When Wilma asked her where she got the recipe, Gran-ma simply shrugged and said she couldn't rightly remember: "I was just using whatever I had in the cupboard."

Obviously, there was a little something extra in that cupboard. Can you guess what it was?

What Gran-ma lacked in décor—what she never even knew about "style"—she made up for, with something far more precious: her love.

There's a simple truth here. Please don't miss it. "Better is a dinner of herbs where love is, than a fatted calf and hatred." (Proverbs 15:17 NKJV) Sounds cryptic? Here's another translation:

"A vegetarian meal served with love is better than a big, thick steak with a plateful of animosity." (Proverbs 15:17 ISV)

The secret ingredient in any good recipe is LOVE.

When served with love, even the simplest, humblest meal turns into a banquet. *What's for dinner?* Same thing we served last night and every day before: *Love.* Whatever you're cooking up today, prepare it lovingly and it will be a culinary masterpiece.

This Christmas, be sure to open your heart and home to those around you. Heed God's command to "Show hospitality to one another...." (1 Peter 4:9 BLB)[13]

Please follow the example of a humble grandmother. Don't stress out over having everything "perfect." Focus instead on the people you invite into your home; on the relationships you're building. Don't worry about preparing (or providing) a fancy meal. There's nothing wrong with sticking with the tried and true. The same dishes you prepare for yourself or your family can easily be shared with guests.

So reach out to someone and share a meal, no matter how simple. Never forget, what you're really serving is love, and that's always gourmet.

Remember those twin pops you ate when you were a kid? You'd break one down the middle to get two single pops, one for you and one for a friend. Didn't they taste so much better when shared? Food and love go together like biscuits 'n' gravy. (Okay, we need to stop making everyone hungry.)

"If you really want to make a friend, go to someone's house and eat with him ... the people who give you their food give you their heart." (Cesar Chavez)

---

[13] Be sure to read the special section on hospitality on page 195.

No Bundt at Christmas!

CHRISTMASTIME IS A PERFECT OCCASION for discussing molds. No, not the fuzzy green ones that grow on very old bread—but rather the kind used to shape stuff, such as Jello.

We have several molds designed to shape different foods, and we have a lot of fun using them. We have a heart-shaped baking pan, and we've used it to bake a meatloaf that screams "LOVE"! We have molds for shaping mounds of rice and chicken salad, making a beautiful presentation when serving these dishes. We have ice cube trays that enable us to freeze punch in a variety of cute shapes. And we have a fish mold, too. So, if our doctor ever tells us to cut out red meat and go on a seafood diet, we'll just bake a meatloaf shaped like a fish.

In addition to all these cool molds, there's also the universally familiar ring-shaped bundt baking pan. The bundt design mimics the form of a traditional European cake called *Gugelhupf*, which was popular with Jewish communities in Germany, Austria and Poland. The first bundt pans were marketed in the U.S. in the late 1950s. The pans quickly caught on, and today you can buy bundt pans in a variety of designs, including cathedrals and city skylines—because who doesn't want to play Godzilla and devour a whole city made of cake?

Interestingly, a Gugelhupf is baked from a *specific*, yeast-based recipe with fruit and nuts. You cannot say the same thing about a bundt cake. In fact, there are no recipes for bundt cake. So, what exactly is a bundt cake? Simple: anything you bake in a bundt pan. It doesn't matter if it's lemon cake or angel-food; if it contains fruit, nuts, or a tunnel of fudge filling; whatever goes into a bundt pan is called a bundt cake. Which provides a perfect analogy for what we want to share.

Although Bundt cakes retain the flavors baked into them, they nevertheless lose part of their identity. Being molded by a bundt pan makes them bundt cakes. A chocolate cake becomes a bundt cake. Same for a yellow cake, a banana cake, or what have you. If cakes could talk they'd probably argue with the cook about being baked in a mold that leads to the loss of their individuality. Can you guess where we're going with this?

People often end up like bundt cakes. They may start out as chocolate, vanilla, yellow or red velvet, but somewhere in life they allow society to mold them into something generic.

Our world is continually pressuring people to conform to a certain image and mindset. Peer pressure is constantly working to mold us; the need to "fit in" or the desire to "keep up with the Joneses" are just two examples of "social bundt pans." And if you're a follower of the God of the Bible, you face even greater pressure to conform to a secular culture. Face it, "bundt people" want you to join their ranks.

The Apostle Paul admonishes us, "Do not conform to the pattern of this world, but be transformed by the renewing of your mind." (Romans 12:2 NIV)

In other words, don't allow this fallen, negative, lost and hopeless world to squeeze you into its mold. Instead, be different, maintain a higher standard, avoid the dog-eat-dog mentality of the rest of society. Be like Christ: never stoop to the low standards of people who are unforgiving and vindictive, unloving and often vicious. Take the high road instead; rise above your circumstances and whatever else the world throws at you; and live by faith.

Get God's perspective on life by reading His Word. Trade in any hopeless, faithless feelings you may have, for God's faithful promises. Replace any negative, hateful, selfish, stinking thinking with the "mind of Christ" and "love, joy, peace, patience, kindness, goodness, faithfulness, gentleness, and self-control." (Galatians 5:22-23 NLT)

As we continue to enjoy Christmastime, we'll probably encounter—amid other holiday goodies such as pecan fudge, gingerbread cookies and plum pudding—our fair share of bundt cakes. When you see one, let it be a silent reminder not to let the world squeeze you into its mold: don't get caught up in the hustle and bustle of shopping, over decorating, and trying to impress people over the holidays. Christmas isn't about competing with the neighbors or impressing the boss. Nor should it become an excuse to overindulge in food or sink deeper in debt at the department stores.

Break out of the mold. Christmas is a time for celebrating the gift of Jesus Christ to the world—with dear friends and family who take comfort in the simplest pleasures of life, the joy of the Lord and the fellowship of good company. And, uh, a cup of eggnog or hot cider, of course.

Don't be a bundt! Be better!

Think different, and live victoriously! "With perfect peace You will protect those whose minds cannot be changed, because they trust You." (Isaiah 26:3 GW)

Candy Canes, Christmas Angels

NOTHING REPRESENTS CHRISTMAS quite like a candy cane. We hang these seasonal candies on our Christmas trees; we decorate our cards and presents with them; and we pass them out to our kids and co-workers (occasionally wondering which group is more mature). We see big foam and cardboard candy canes on floats in parades, adorning the doors of department stores, clinging to street lamps in our shopping districts; and if we watch holiday classics such as *Miracle on 34th Street* or *How the Grinch Stole Christmas*, we see candy canes pop up in numerous scenes.

Face it, everyone knows a candy cane practically sings out "Merry Christmas!" But there's far more the candy cane wishes to communicate: an unspoken and, at one time, *secret* message about the story behind Christmas.

We've written about several of the foods and kitchen items that "speak" to us in roundabout ways. In observing how we all respond to different aspects of dining, or through working with the many gadgets that facilitate cooking, or by living with the often, idiosyncratic appliances which populate every home, we've discovered more than a few similarities between people and this host of kitchen angels.

But concerning the candy cane, no creative analogies need be drawn to illustrate a Biblical truth; because the candy cane was actually *designed* to convey a singular message—but discreetly, lest someone take offense at the message. In fact, the candy cane is not only one of the very first "angels in the kitchen," but also an "undercover" angel!

The candy cane was invented by a confectioner in Cologne, Germany, in 1670, under the directions of the choirmaster at Cologne Cathedral. The clergyman had been looking for ways to keep the children in his church calm and quiet during the Living Crèche tradition on Christmas Eve. He eventually decided a long-lasting stick of hard peppermint candy might pacify his restless "babes." But passing out candy during a worship service wasn't exactly an appropriate or acceptable practice.

To justify serving candy in church, the choirmaster asked a local candy maker to shape and color the sweet treat in a manner that would remind kids of the ministry of their Savior. Hence, the candy cane would become a Bible study teaching aid—perfectly acceptable in a house of worship. So, here now, for your edification (drumroll, please) are the many lessons taught by the candy cane:

Because the stick of candy has a crook at the top, it resembles a shepherd's staff. This shape reminds children of the poor shepherds, in the Christmas story, who visited the infant Jesus; of the knowledge that the Heavenly Father is the Good Shepherd; and the revelation that Christ came to gather up God's people and shepherd them back to the Father. (John 10:11; see also Psalm 23.)

The snow white base-color of the candy cane reminds children (of all ages) of the purity of Jesus the Messiah: Christ shared all our human weaknesses when He walked the earth, and he faced the same temptations with which we struggle daily; and yet, He led a sinless life—which uniquely qualified our Lord as a perfect sacrifice for the atonement of our sins, "a lamb without spot or wrinkle"! (1 Peter 1:19)

The traditional candy cane is marked by three thin red lines and one bold red band. The three scarlet stripes remind us that, about 2000 years ago, Jesus was scourged for our iniquities—and by His stripes we are healed. (Isaiah 53:5)

The thick red band surrounding the cane represents the blood Christ shed that day, when He was sacrificed on a Roman cross at Calvary—the cleansing and redeeming blood of Christ which paid the full penalty for our sins, and which surrounds and covers every believer. (See Psalm 51:7)

There are exactly three thin stripes to represent the divine presence and power of the Trinity of God, the Father, the Son, and the Holy Spirit, all working on behalf of anyone who trusts in Jesus.

Legend also tells that during a time of great Christian persecution during the latter half of the eighteenth century, believers used the candy cane as a means of discreetly identifying themselves: at a time when wearing crosses was forbidden, and any open display of faith in Christ or identification with Christians beliefs might result in death, believers relied on the mute message of the simple candy cane to express what was in their hearts.

The candy cane, God's Christmas Angel in the Kitchen, stills bears greetings from our Lord throughout the holidays, as well as an important truth: that something insignificant, like a piece of hard candy—or a person who has made mistakes (and perhaps even continues to make mistakes)—can be transformed into something of great significance and value.

So, the next time you see a candy cane, remember it doesn't just represent Christmas, it tells the story *behind* Christmas.

"And in the same region there were shepherds out in the field, keeping watch over their flock by night. And an angel of the Lord appeared to them, and ... said to them, 'Fear not, for behold, I bring you good news of great joy that will be for all the people. For unto you is born this day in the city of David a Savior, who is Christ the Lord.'" (Luke 2:8-10 ESV)

170

The Christmas Catastrophe

HI, I'M KERRI, an *InSinkErator*.

Having trouble pronouncing my name? Say, "Er-ā-ter." Now say "In-Sink-Erator." Now say it fast!

I beg your pardon!!! I am NOT a garbage disposal! I do help my pals Tom and Wilma with kitchen cleanup, by getting rid of coffee grounds and other food scraps—but I'd never confess to eating garbage. Would you? No matter. I'm here to share with you the story of the Christmas Catastrophe.

How well I remember it. It happened many years ago, in another kitchen. Wilma was deep-frying a batch of tasty egg rolls for our annual Christmas open-house. At least, I *think* they were delicious. No one ever gave me a piece to sample. All of the guests enthusiastically wolfed them down, leaving behind nothing for me but an occasional lemon slice from a well-drained glass of ice tea. Oops, enough about me.

After deep frying her crispy egg rolls, Wilma made a real *boo-boo!* Without thinking, she poured the super-heated oil from her deep fryer down my gullet. I tried to warn her—

I was yawning at the time, because hanging out in the sink can get pretty boring—but I never got a chance. As many of you know by now, just about everything in the kitchen has a message to relate, which is why Tom and Wilma affectionately refer to us as angels. But what happened next left me speechless. One minute I'm daydreaming, the next I have a mouthful of boiling oil. And, well, you're not supposed to talk with your mouth full.

What made things worse was that the oil wouldn't go down. I already had some discarded celery and onion pieces caught in my throat. I needed to cough and politely clear my throat, and then inform Wilma that it's not good to pour "grease" down the drain—especially grease approaching the temperature of molten lava.

Too late! To my horror, Wilma flipped my switch, and like an erupting volcano, I spewed out red-hot oil—right in her face! I heard her cry out, as she quickly, and blindly, turned on the faucet and repeatedly splashed her seared face with cold water. She was careful to gently pat her face, and not to rub her scalded skin or burning eyes. To her credit, she stayed calm, despite thoughts that she'd blinded herself.

I wish I could say the same about Tom. At first, he panicked. But then he handled it, and quickly drove his wife to the emergency room.

The ER doctor flushed her eyes, and applied a thick white ointment all over her face, which made her look like Casper the Friendly Ghost. He said she had second- and third-degree burns around her eyes, and that she was lucky there was no eye damage. To which Wilma gently responded, "Not lucky, but blessed! God protected my eyes."

The doctor smiled and gave her an antibiotic, which was wise, because later she ran a low-grade fever, and then Tom drove her back home. Along the way, he glanced over at her blistered and swollen face, and said "We'll have to cancel our gathering." *But they didn't!* That evening, Wilma greeted their guests with a face covered in white glop and missing half of one eyebrow. She wanted their guests to celebrate with her; she'd been wounded in the line of kitchen duty, but according to the doctor, she wouldn't be permanently scarred. Best of all, *she could see(!)*—all the ugly Christmas sweaters their guests were wearing.

Today you'd never know Wilma was wounded in the kitchen: she has no scars, and no fear of frying. Oh, sure, she's still missing a tiny piece of one eyebrow, but I think it gives her character.

Interestingly, most accidents in the home occur in the kitchen. As Tom and Wilma frequently state, the kitchen is the heart of the home; and it's filled with sharp objects and lots of stuff that can burn. People have gotten cut, pierced, spattered and singed. But do their kitchen accidents and mistakes drive them away from cooking? Nope. Their less fortunate experiences only tend to make them more careful and a little wiser.

Life is like cooking. And like the kitchen, the human heart can be filled with things that cut, pierce, and blister. Disappointments and failures can wound like a chef's knife. A betrayal, a divorce, or a broken relationship; an accident, an illness, or a financial setback; a bad decision, a mistake, or an indiscretion—can all be emotionally wounding.

Face it, at one time or another, everyone gets burnt by something in life. Sometimes, however, it's our own lack of wisdom or carelessness that leads to suffering. But God doesn't want our mishaps and emotional wounds to keep us from enjoying life. If you're bleeding over a severed relationship, don't allow your wounds to keep you from trusting people and forming new friendships. If you've been blistered by a bum deal, or you're stinging from a stupid mistake, don't allow the pain to keep you from moving forward. God can heal all the wounds of the human heart, while forgiving our own shortcomings, mistakes and failures —if we let Him.

When it first happened, Wilma's careless goof literally brought tears to her eyes. But she trusted God to heal her. As a result, she can now look back on "The Christmas

Catastrophe" and smile. Because God is faithful, and time can heal all wounds. And when the time is used wisely ... "The nights of crying your eyes out give way to days of laughter." (Psalm 30:5 MSG).

Have you been burnt in life? Although it hurts now, you'll eventually heal, just like Wilma's seared face. Give God time to heal your heart, but put the time to good use. Don't withdraw from life and relationships. Remain involved with people and activities.

Above all, spend a significant amount of your healing time with the Lord in prayer. Jesus Christ can definitely relate to you, because He "...was despised and rejected—a man of sorrows, acquainted with deepest grief." (Isaiah 53:3 NLT) And He's faithful to heal all your hurts: "He heals the brokenhearted and binds up their wounds." (Psalm 147:3 NIV)

Show God your emotional cuts, burns, and bruises. Ask him to heal your heart. Trust in His power and faithfulness, and then move forward in life. God will not only heal you, He'll also ensure your heart isn't permanently scarred. You'll soon be back in the "kitchen of life" and cooking up great things.

Not a Fruitcake!

CONCERNING FRUITCAKES, apparently more people enjoy baking them than eating them. Why else do fruitcakes constantly show up beneath the Christmas tree or in a game of White Elephant? Because at least one cook in every family bakes several each year with the good intentions of distributing them as gifts. In fact, fruitcakes are to Christmas what toasters are to weddings.

So, as we sip eggnog with friends and family by the fireside, someone will inevitably pass us a suspicious looking loaf-shaped parcel tied up with a bow. With a little trepidation, we slowly unwrap our gift. Is it another necktie? Socks? A high-def TV? No, it's a dense hunk of nuts and gummy fruit barely held together by a pinch of flour and a hasty prayer. Ho Ho Ho—*oooh!*

Oh, thanks! But you shouldn't have. NO, seriously, you shouldn't have!

And now it begins: the annual fruitcake shuffle. We pass it off to you, you pawn it off on your boss, your boss re-gifts it to his sister, she takes it to her pastor, he delivers it to a board member who's been a pain in his neck, the pain-in-the-neck gives it to his neighbor who babysits for him when she's actually got better things to do—and who deserves something much nicer for the time she's spent—and she ... uh, just happens to know us.

This poor, overtaxed servant brings it right back to us: "Hi, I couldn't get out and do any shopping—'cuz I've been babysitting a lot of nights—but look, I brought you guys a fruitcake!!"

"Oh, yummy!" we cry in unison, giving her a hug. "You really, *really* shouldn't have!"

Once our guest departs, one of us asks, "Sweetie, isn't this the same fruitcake we got rid of a few days ago?"

"Could be," the reply comes. "Then again, you never know: after all, all fruitcakes look alike to me."

"I hope it's not the same one we gave away last year. Ya know, some of these things should be subjected to carbon-dating. So, what should we do?"

"Don't we still need to give your brother a gift?"

For a long, awkward moment we stare at each other in silence. How could we stoop so low? We should be ashamed of ourselves. We should be....

"Yeah, why not."

Before we continue with this confessional, we'd like to ask a nagging question: Does anyone ever buy a fruitcake? Probably not. Because everyone knows that someone somewhere has one they're trying to give away. Actually, legend has it that there are only a finite number of fruit-cakes still in existence, all of them baked centuries ago by trolls living under a bridge. These dried out blocks of fruit and nuts just stay in circulation ... making the rounds ... the quintessential objects of re-gifting ... forever ... and ever ... Hallelujah ... Hallelujah! *Sigh!*

There's a scientific theory that should anyone—let's say, someone who's delirious from hunger—ever actually consume one, it would start a chain-reaction that could usher in the end of civilization as we know it. But not to worry, Christmas is just around the corner. And fruitcakes are the gift that keeps on giving. Year after year after year.

There's another gift that keeps on giving—but not be-cause anyone re-gifts it. In fact, no one who's ever received this gift has ever wanted to part with it—it's that precious. No one can make it, and no one can buy it. It can't be earned and it can't be given away. It's the free gift of eternal life, bestowed by our Heavenly Father, through His Son Jesus Christ. "The payment for sin is death, but the gift that God freely gives is everlasting life found in Christ Jesus our Lord." (Romans 6:23 GW)

Whenever they could break into someone's kitchen, velociraptors were notorious for baking deadly, prehistoric fruitcakes.
(image: *Jurassic Park* copyright 1993 by Universal Studios)

Christmas commemorates the day Jesus Christ (the Jewish Messiah Yeshua) came to earth in human-form; the birth of the Savior of the world, in a Bethlehem manger over 2000 years ago, as predicted by the prophet Isaiah: "For unto us a child is born, unto us a Son is given...." (Isaiah 9:6 KJV)

It's a time of giving gifts, because the arrival of Christ on earth led to His giving the greatest gift mankind has ever known—or ever will. Christ gave His life for each of us. "Thanks be to God for his indescribable gift!" (2 Corinthians 9:15 NIV)

Have you opened God's gift yet? Trust us, that's no fruitcake—or anything else you'd want to give away. Indeed, it's a treasure that keeps on giving throughout eternity. "If you declare with your mouth, 'Jesus is Lord,' and believe in your heart that God raised Him from the dead, you will be saved." (Romans 10:9 NIV)

God saved you by His grace when you believed. And you can't take credit for this. It is a gift from God.
—Ephesians 2:8 NLT

177

Boiling It Down

WE RECENTLY DISCOVERED that Stacy, one of our oldest kitchen angels, is *full* of wisdom. *Literally.*

Stacy is our faithful stockpot. She's been with us all our married life—37 happy years. In fact—Stacy Stockpot was a wedding gift. Oh, *excuse us*, she insists she was a wedding *guest*.

There are two things Stacy loves most in this world, making soup and keeping us in suspense. Allow us to explain. One day, while cooking a batch of chicken soup, Stacy decided to tease us with a series of intriguing questions:

"Do you know why your moms and grandmas served you chicken soup when you were kids and you were coming down with a cold?" She asks.

No, Stacy, why was that?

"Do you know why chicken soup has been called the Jewish mother's Penicillin?"

No, Stacy, please tell us.

"Did you know that at one time chicken soup with matzah balls was served everyday in the commissary at MGM Studios, and that it was prepared according to an old family recipe that came from studio head Louis B. Mayer's mom?"

Uh, no, Stacy. That's really interesting, but please tell us *why*.

"Do you know why chicken soup is the universal remedy for colds, the flu, and other ailments?" Or why patients recovering in hospitals are routinely served this culinary cure?

Sigh! Clearly, our faithful stockpot, who's usually full of broth and veggies, is full of knowledge, too. And on this particular day, she's acting like she's also a bit full of herself.

We respond, *Because it's good for you?*

"But *why* is chicken soup good for you? Do you know?"

Not really. Will you *please* tell us already and stop holding us in suspense!

"Okay, okay," Stacy says. "Simmer down and I'll tell you."

Trust us, you've never quite been scolded until a *stockpot* tells you to *simmer* down!

Finally, Stacy began to spill the beans—not actually, we're happy to say, because we had just cleaned the range top—by stating what all our kitchen angels know well: "My people are destroyed for lack of knowledge...." (Hosea 3:6 KJB) This verse refers to a lack of knowledge (or full understanding) of God's Word (the Bible) and its truths; but an ignorance of other pertinent information can destroy our health, happiness and, in general, the "abundant life" Jesus promises us in John 10:10.

Our faithful stockpot then proceeded to tell us *every-thing* she knows about chicken soup. But never fear, dear reader. We asked Stacy to "boil it down" to a few paragraphs we can easily share with you. She agreed, of course. After all, boiling things down—reducing them to their concentrated essence is what a stockpot does best.

The word *essence* means: the key quality or element of a thing; an extract containing all those requisite qualities in concentrated form. From the same root word, we get *essential,* meaning *indispensable,* as in the one indispensable quality or characteristic that makes a thing precisely what it is.

As with soup, written and verbal information can be "boiled down" to *its* essence. We can "reduce" a subject or a situation or an important issue to reach the indispensable heart of the matter. In other words, *to get the gist*.

Stacy prefers the word *essence*. And regarding the subject of chicken soup.... Having just boiled down a fresh batch of the broth, she can now reveal the answers to all her questions concerning the health benefits of "Jewish Mother's Penicillin"! The very *essence* of chicken soup and the reason why it's good for you is:

COLLAGEN

Collagen is the main structural protein comprising the connective tissues in our bodies. It's the basic building blocks for our skin, hair, joints, bones, and even our brains. In fact, collagen accounts for 90 percent of the protein in the human body. Is it *essential* for good health? You betcha! Does the average person get enough collagen in his or her diet? Nope!

At one time, people routinely got more collagen in their diet because they consumed more broths, including chicken soup. Back in the day, our moms and dads prepared chicken soup by tossing veggies, seasonings, and the parts of a cut-up chicken into a stockpot. And because our parents were not wasteful, they used practically everything the bird had to offer except the beak—including the bones. And when they cooked a stew or a pot of beans, they were liable to throw in a nice big ham or beef bone. This was a good thing indeed, because meat bones are an excellent source of collagen. But to get to the essence of these bones, you have to allow the soup to boil down, releasing the collagen and its health benefits, and concentrating them in the broth.

So, again, boiling it down, we find that collagen, with its healing properties, is the essence of both chicken soup—and why this particular broth is good for you. By the way, if you're not into making homemade soup, you can now purchase collagen powders wherever vitamins and other supplements are sold. We do this and add a scoop to our smoothies.

There's something else that can be boiled down—the teachings of the Hospitable God of the Bible; the God of Abraham, Isaac and Israel—in order to render these truths to their essence, and reveal their single, indispensable characteristic.

Jesus did precisely this.

When asked what is the greatest commandment, He responded, "'Love the Lord your God with all your heart and with all your soul and with all your mind.' This is the first and greatest commandment." (Matt 22:37-38 NIV)

Jesus (or Rabbi Yeshua, as He is known by our Jewish friends) was quoting from Deuteronomy 6:5, which is part of the daily prayer, or *Shema*, spoken by Jews even to this day. In so doing, Yeshua was boiling down the first three of the Ten Commandments, which deal with our relationship with God. (See Exodus 20 for The Ten Commandments.)

The Lord then said, "And the second is like it: 'Love your neighbor as yourself.' All the Law and the Prophets hang on [depend on] these two commandments." (Matt 22:38 NIV) Here, Yeshua was referring back to Leviticus 19:18, in order to summarize the remaining seven of the Ten Commandments, all of which deal with our relationships to our fellow human beings.

Jesus Christ took the meat of His Holy Word—the "flesh and bones" of all of Gods commandments—and boiled it down for us. He rendered it to its essence, to its one indispensable ingredient:

LOVE

This is a fitting truth, for the Apostle John writes, "Dear friends, let us love one another, for love comes from God. Everyone who loves has been born of God and knows God. Whoever does not love does not know God, because God is love." (1 John 4:7-8 NIV)

We are commanded to love God and to love other people. And the Apostle Paul describes *how* we are to love them, in 1 Corinthians 13, which is often called the Love chapter. Read it again today.

Let's take stock of this indispensable truth: Love is the essence of God and His Word, and it's vital for enjoying a healthy, happy, and fruitful life.

For information used in this article, we wish to acknowledge the websites of the nutritionists Dr. Don Colbert (DrColbert.com) and Jordan Ruben (AncientNutrition.com); and Joan Nathan's book *Jewish Cooking in America.*

How Do You Smell?

SOME FOODS HAVE SUCH distinctive aromas that we can instantly identify them by smell alone. For instance, the essences of vanilla, bananas, and cinnamon are strong scents that are hard to mask. Of course, vanilla and cinnamon are so pleasant most of us wouldn't want to cover their smell. In fact, many people use these scents to freshen their rooms.

Not all kitchen smells, however, lend themselves to deodorizer scents. It's easy to find vanilla or cinnamon-scented candles and sprays at any store, but good luck finding "boiled collards"! Some smells do nothing to freshen the atmosphere. Fried fish and chicken curry may taste good, but their odors (notice we didn't write aromas) are strong repellents.

Most fresh cooked foods are powerful attractants, though. Throw a steak on the grill and there's a good chance your neighbor will walk over to say hello. Bring home a steaming pizza, and everyone in the house will suddenly feel hungry—for pizza. Indeed, people are attracted to certain smells. Place a steaming meal on the table and you probably won't need to ring the dinner bell—your family will be lured by the appetite-arousing aroma.

God greatly blessed us when He gave us the sense of smell, because our world is redolent with a multitude of fragrances. Even people smell.

Uh, that didn't exactly come out right. We're not referring to BO. Nor are we referring to a lady's Chanel #5 or a gentleman's aftershave. Granted, some people are recognizable by the perfume or cologne they use, but the smell we'd like to discuss here is of a spiritual nature. Smells communicate powerful messages to the brain: they can make us hungry or cause us to lose our appetites; attract or repulse us; put us in a relaxed mood or make us feel anxious.

Previously we discussed the "essence" of God. It's LOVE, the "soothing aroma" of Christ's sacrifice on the cross, which paid the penalty for our sins. (John 3:16) The Apostle Paul wrote, "Live a life filled with love, following the example of Christ. He loved us and offered Himself as a sacrifice for us, a pleasing aroma to God." (Ephesians 5:2 NLT)

God's signature fragrance is love, and in a manner of speaking, Paul admonishes us to "smell" like God. Okay, we know you can't really smell love, but God wants us to emit love the way a spice cake emits the delicious aroma of cinnamon, cloves and nutmeg. He wants us to draw people to His Divine Table the same way the smell of pizza draws us to the kitchen table. So comparing God's love to a pleasing scent is actually an excellent analogy.

"...I thank God, who always leads us in victory because of Christ. Wherever we go, God uses us to make clear what it means to know Christ. It's like a fragrance that fills the air." (2 Corinthians 2:14 GW)

Every believer should smell like the Love of Christ (the Bread of Life). When we walk into a room, people should immediately be able to detect the comforting aroma—a fragrance that will attract them and make them hungry for the things of God. "...If I am lifted up from the earth I will draw all people to Myself." (John 12:32 HCSB)

Of course, many of us don't always have this particular scent. Instead, we often reek of self-serving indifference or— far more foul—the stink of hatred. But we're called to be God's ambassadors to a lost and hurting world—His loving hands extended in friendship and service. So, touch a life. Put on Christ (Galatians 3:27) and fill the atmosphere—at home, school, work, and wherever else God takes you— with the sweet aroma of God's Love (which is the essence of 1 Corinthians 13).

By the way, how do you smell?

The Hospitable Pineapple

ANYONE WHO'S VISITED OUR HOME knows we're crazy about birds! The walls in nearly every room are adorned with framed prints depicting blue jays, woodpeckers, cardinals and herons, to name a few. But there's another decorating theme running through Woodhaven: pineapples.

We have friends in Hawaii who continue to send us gifts of handcrafted bowls, spoons and plaques featuring this giant golden fruit, but recently one of them jokingly proclaimed, "You guys need to pick another theme!" She said they had just about exhausted all the tchotchkes that are available in the "Pineapple State." *Aloha!*

So why are we crazy over pineapples? We have the design mounted above the entrances to our foyer and kitchen, on the wall next to our French doors, etched on goblets and mugs, and imprinted on coasters and dinnerware. Pineapples adorn our candlesticks and napkin rings, our serving pieces and—best of all—the centerpiece we place on the table each year at Christmastime. And as if these decorations weren't enough, one of us greets our guests wearing tiny gold pineapple earrings. (Hint: it's not Tom.)

One of these guests, a teenager named Nicolas, who was visiting with his parents, spent nearly an entire weekend wandering about the rooms at Woodhaven counting all the pineapples he came across, including a few crafted into the antique furniture. Trust us, his imaginative little game of "Find the Pineapples" kept Nicolas busy for hours. That's not to say, however, that the inside of our home looks like something out of Charles Dickens' *The Old Curiosity Shop*. We try to ... *ahem* ... maintain a modicum of good taste and sensible order at Woodhaven.

Nevertheless, Nicolas finally asked quite politely, "What's up with all the pineapples?" To answer this question, we need to return to the Colonial Days of America. No, we don't need a time machine, we can get there by car. We live within easy driving distance of the first capital of Virginia: Colonial Williamsburg, where the past of over 250 years ago is daily re-enacted in our country's largest outdoor museum.

As we stroll down the streets of Williamsburg we see ... pineapples—*lots* of pineapples—on and above the doors, decorating signs and wreaths, imprinted on tourist maps and brochures, and in every gift and souvenir shop. In fact, the pineapple is one of the official symbols of this Colonial town, because the fruit has an interesting place in its early history.

Christopher Columbus had discovered the pineapple on his second trip to the Caribbean in 1493. He took the spiky-skinned fruit back to Spain where it became both a novelty food and a sign of status and wealth. Europeans weren't able to grow the fruit. At least, not until the first hothouses were constructed—and those were only built on the grandest estates. So the tropical delicacy had to be imported from the Caribbean; and the fruit had to survive the long humid trip across the Atlantic. Much of the fruit rotted before reaching its destination, but the pineapples that did make it to European tables were rare and expensive indeed!

In Colonial Williamsburg, England's headquarters in America during the 1700s, pineapples continued to be viewed as luxury items. Whenever the fruit arrived on a British merchant ship, a prosperous host or hostess would quickly send a buyer in the hope of claiming one of the scarce fruits. When he or she succeeded, they would place the exotic fruit at the center of the dining table, where all the guests could admire it. At the conclusion of the meal, the pineapple was carved and served to the guests, who considered the rare and expensive fruit the ultimate expression of their host's hospitality.

Hence, the pineapple soon became the symbol of sincere and abundant hospitality, proclaiming: *"Welcome!"; "Aloha!"; "¡Bienvenidos!"; "Shalom!"*—and we're all for hospitality! In fact, we've written a book on the subject, *The Heart of an Angel,* the first in a series about the sacred practice of hospitality.[14] We sincerely believe that if people everywhere were more hospitable, we could solve most of the ills of our world.

Besides, our Heavenly Father, actually *commands* us to be hospitable: "Be hospitable to one another without complaint." (1 Peter 4:9 NASB) Or to put it another way, "Cheerfully share your home with those who need a meal or a place to stay." (1 Peter 4:9 NLT)

Why?

Because our Heavenly Father, the God of Abraham, Isaac and Israel, is first and foremost a HOSPITABLE God.

And the Hospitable God of the Bible longs for us to be more like Him: *loving, caring, giving, accepting, affirming,* and ... *welcoming!* Indeed, "God so *loved* the world that He *gave* His only Son, that *whosoever* believes in Him should not perish, but have everlasting life." (John 3:16)

In the ultimate act of hospitality, our Heavenly Father sent His only Son to earth, to die for our sins, thereby redeeming us, in order to *welcome* us back to Him. And two thousand years later God still invites all of us *whosoevers* to take our place at His Heavenly Table; by

---

[14] Publisher's Note: Learn more about the sacred practice of hospitality, one of the most neglected and misunderstood concepts in our society today, by reading an excerpt of Tom and Wilma's book *The Heart of an Angel: Becoming God's Messengers of Love and Hospitality to a World in Need,* included as a special bonus preview, beginning on page 195.

believing in Him and following His hospitable example of *loving, giving, and ... serving.*

But serving is never easy, or convenient, or timely!

Welcoming a new neighbor by inviting them to your home for a meal—or simply coffee and conversation—may not fit into your busy schedule. Visiting a sick or injured coworker in the hospital may take you miles out of your way. And taking a covered dish to an elderly or disabled shut-in will take extra effort and planning. Such acts of kind service seldom come naturally, because...

Serving almost always involves sacrifice. But again, we should follow the example of the Hospitable God of the Bible, who sacrificed His only begotten Son in order to save us.

And we can learn from the Son, also. Following His Father's hospitable example, Jesus Christ proclaimed "...The Son of Man did not come to be served, but to serve, and to give His life a ransom for many." (Matthew 20:28 NASB)

Jesus literally *sacrificed* everything to *serve* us. In essence, He served up His very life. Together, the Father and the Son, sacrificing supremely and serving others in love, give us a clear picture of what it means to be hospitable. They are our great examples, and the inspiration for our personal definition of the sacred practice of hospitality.

HOSPITALITY IS AN *ATTITUDE* OF THE HEART (LOVE) EXPRESSED THROUGH A *LIFESTYLE* OF GIVING AND SERVING. IT'S THE GIVING OF YOUR TIME, TALENTS AND RESOURCES. IT'S THE GIVING OF YOURSELF.

So how 'bout it? Ready to invite the new neighbors to dinner? Or to take a covered dish to that single parent? Hey, practicing hospitality may not always be convenient or easy, but it's always personally rewarding and truly worthwhile—because through these acts of kindness, you'll be touching lives and making a difference. You will indeed be making our world a better (more hospitable) place in which to live. And every time you're hospitable, your Heavenly Father will see ... and remark:

"Well done, good and faithful <u>servant</u>!" (Matt 25:21 NIV)

Dear friends, it's our heartfelt prayer that whenever you see or eat a pineapple you'll be reminded to be hospitable. You'll be glad you did.

Pineapples, Pain, and the Power of Hospitality

THE PINEAPPLE AND HOSPITALITY: both let people know they are welcome.

Hospitable people open their hearts and homes to others. They are sensitive to the needs of those around them, and they make room in their lives for the people they encounter on the highways and byways of life. And, as previously discussed, the pineapple has come to symbolize the sacred practice of hospitality.

That's why the pineapple motif appears throughout our

home. We want our guests to feel welcomed at Woodhaven. And hey! Wanna know what's really neat about hospitality and the pineapple?

Pineapple contains a unique protein enzyme known as bromelain, an all-natural pain reliever. In fact, savvy surgeons often recommend their patients eat or juice a fresh pineapple to aid their recovery after surgery. This unique medicinal property of the pineapple further makes it a fitting symbol of hospitality, and a reminder not to neglect its practice; because when you welcome people into your own home, your act of hospitality goes a long ways to relieving the pain of isolation, loneliness and discouragement.

Indeed, we get the term *hospitality* from the Latin word *hospitalis*. We also take our idea of "hospital" from this Latin word, which is wholly appropriate: a hospital is a place of *healing* and *restoration*, and these concerns are the true focus of hospitality.

When we practice hospitality, opening up our hearts and homes to others, we become God's conduit of healing and restoration. We become His hands extended, and our homes become mini-hospitals, providing an oasis of rest and refreshment in a mostly inhospitable world.

Some might say, "*My* house is my *home*—not a clinic for troubled people! No less an authority than the Apostle Paul counters with the commandment "Share each other's burdens, and in this way obey the law of Christ." (Galatians 6:2 NLT) In other words, "Share each other's troubles and problems, and so obey our Lord's command." (TLB)

Enjoying a good meal and pleasant company is always fun, and such things are certainly facets of hospitality; but the main purpose of the sacred practice is to establish, develop, and nurture meaningful relationships—both with God and our fellow travelers in life. Hospitality goes far beyond hanging out with friends and family; it's about tearing down walls that divide us, and building bridges between people who otherwise don't "connect"; it's about arranging those "divine connections" through which individuals are able to find common ground and share their burdens, and God is able to restore and repair.

The Jewish people have a Hebrew phrase, *tikkun olam* (or *tikkun ha-olum*), which expresses the idea of having a personal responsibility to repair and improve the world we live in. The concept implies that our world is "broken" and in need of repair—which is consistent with the Biblical truth of "the Fall of Man" as recorded in Genesis—and that it's up to God's people to repair it. Which takes us back to the Apostle Paul's admonishment to bear one another's burdens; "For we are of God's making," he writes in Ephesians 2:10, "created in union with the Messiah Yeshua for a life of good actions already prepared by God for us to do." (Complete Jewish Bible)

Plainly speaking, we are mandated by the Hospitable God of the Bible to do everything we can to make a better world. One very simple but highly effective way we can all work to accomplish this is by engaging in the sacred practice of hospitality, thus becoming His heart and hands, reaching out and expressing His love in practical ways.

There's no better way of addressing and meeting needs than by practicing hospitality, particularly in our homes. Although we can and should be hospitable wherever we go, the home is the best venue. It provides the safest and most private environment, where people can feel free to open up and share what's on their heart. Indeed, the home is the one place we don't have to put on a "happy face"; where we can remove our everything-is-wonderful masks and be honest and transparent.

Furthermore, when you practice hospitality you will encounter all sorts of "angels"! Biblically speaking, angels were heavenly messengers God sent to earth. But the people God daily sends your way also have a "message" to deliver. Each and every one of us has a story to tell, an experience to relate, a new perspective to bring to the table. And because we each have a unique upbringing, background, life experiences, and spiritual journey, it's a message that only you and I can share. Face it, *life* is a message, and we are its messengers.

Heed the words of Hebrews 13:1-2, which admonish us, "Keep on loving one another as brothers and sisters. Do not forget to show hospitality to strangers, for by so doing some people have shown hospitality to angels without knowing it." (NIV) This scripture is actually referencing back to the Patriarch Abraham and his supernatural encounter with three *Heavenly* messengers, a trio of *real* angels, as recorded in Genesis 18. By the way, Abraham, the Father of Faith, is also the Biblical icon of the sacred practice of hospitality. He's our role model.

So please consider opening your heart and home to those around you, especially during holidays—and not just your family members. Extend your social circle beyond your friends and relatives. Reach out to your neighbors, coworkers, and the members of your community who often get left out of things: singles and people who have lost loved ones; military spouses whose husbands and wives are serving away from home; college students who can't make it home for the weekend; shut-ins, who spend most of their days in isolation; and anyone else you happen to meet who can use a little love and reassurance.

Maybe you'll even serve them some fresh pineapple, the hospitable fruit.

Wilma Espaillat English grew up in a bilingual, bicultural family in New York and New Jersey, learning firsthand the significance of hospitality in the Hispanic culture. Today she is a published writer, speaker and educator. She has taught a variety of subjects at both high school and college levels, including Spanish and Ancient World History. She has written high school curriculum for classes in Multicultural Studies from a Judeo-Christian perspective, and conducted seminars for civic groups, including law enforcement agencies. She has also taught Bible and Christian Life topics to adults of all ages. She's the wife of Tom English.

Tom English grew up in a "Southern fried" family in rural Virginia. Today he is a Senior Chemist at Newport News Ship-building. He is also a published writer and an award-nominated editor of both fiction and nonfiction. His fantasy and adventure stories have appeared in various magazines and several print anthologies, including *Haunted House Short Stories, Detective Thrillers Short Stories,* and *Gaslight Arcanum: Uncanny Tales of Sherlock Holmes.* Tom also edited the mammoth hardcover *Bound for Evil: Curious Tales of Books Gone Bad,* a 2008 Shirley Jackson Award finalist for best anthology. He is currently the editor of the retro-flavored science fiction magazine *Black Infinity.* Like his wife, Wilma, he has extensive knowledge in Biblical Studies and has taught Christian Life classes to both singles and married couples of all ages. He resides with Wilma, surrounded by books and beasts, deep in the woods of New Kent, Virginia.

Tom and Wilma invite you to join them each weekday for humorous and inspiring new articles at their internet home, www.AngelAtTheDoor.com

LIST OF BIBLE TRANSLATIONS CITED

AKJV - *Authorized King James Version,* Cambridge University Press

AMP - *The Amplified Bible*, The Lockman Foundation (2015).

AMPC - *The Amplified Bible: Classic Edition*, Lockman Foundation (1987)

BLB - *Berean Literal Bible*, Bible Hub (2016)

BSB - *Berean Study Bible*, Bible Hub (2016)

CEB - *Common English Bible*, Common English Bible (2011)

CEV - *Contemporary English Version*, American Bible Society (1995)

CJB - David Stern, *Complete Jewish Bible* (1998)

CSB - *Christian Standard Bible*, Holman Bible Publishers (2017)

EHV - *Evangelical Heritage Version*, The Wartburg Project (2017)

ERV - *Easy-to-Read Version*, World Bible Translation Center (2006)

ESV - *The English Standard Version*, Crossway Bibles (2001)

EXB - *The Expanded Bible*, Thomas Nelson Inc. (2011)

GNT - *Good News Translation,* American Bible Society (1992)

GW - *God's Word*, God's Word to the Nations (1995)

HCSB - *Holman Christian Standard Bible*, Holman Bible Publishers (2003)

ICB - *International Children's Bible*, Thomas Nelson (2015)

ISV - *International Standard Version*, ISV Foundation (1996-2012)

JUB - *Jubilee Bible*, Life Sentence Publishing (2000, 2001, 2010)

KJV - *King James Version* (1611; revised 1769)

KJ21 - *21st Century King James Version,* Deuel Enterprises, Inc. (1994)

MSG - *The Message,* E. H. Peterson (2002)

NASB - *New American Standard Bible*, Lockman Foundation (1995)

NCV - *New Century Version*, Thomas Nelson, Inc. (2005)

NET - *The NET Bible*/New English Trans., Biblical Studies Press (2005)

NIV - *The New International Version*, Biblica, Inc. (1984, 2011)

NKJV - *New King James Version*, Thomas Nelson, Inc. (1982)

NLT - *New Living Translation*, Tyndale House Foundation (1996, 2007)

NOG - *The Names of God Bible*, Baker Publishing Group (2011)

PHILLIPS - J. B. Phillips, *The New Testament in Modern English* (1958)

TLB - *The Living Bible,* Kenneth Taylor (1971)

VOICE - *The Voice Bible,* Thomas Nelson; Ecclesia Bible Society (2012)

WNT - Richard Francis Weymouth, *Weymouth New Testament* (1903)

A SPECIAL PREVIEW OF

THE
HEART OF AN ANGEL

BECOMING GOD'S MESSENGERS OF LOVE
AND HOSPITALITY TO A WORLD IN NEED!

TOM ENGLISH AND
WILMA ESPAILLAT ENGLISH

RAVENS'
READS

AN IMPRINT OF DEAD LETTER PRESS
BOX 134, NEW KENT, VA 23124-0134

THIS SPECIAL PREVIEW OF
THE HEART OF AN ANGEL
COPYRIGHT © 2016 AND 2020
BY TOM ENGLISH AND
WILMA ESPAILLAT ENGLISH

INTRODUCTION:
BAND OF ANGELS!

After [Jesus] had fasted forty days and forty nights, He was hungry. ...And immediately angels came and began to serve Him.

—Matthew 4:2, 11 (Holman CSB)

THROUGHOUT BIBLICAL TIMES GOD used an army of celestial beings to make special announcements, and to minister to His people on earth. These supernatural beings frequently visited our mortal world in the guise of strangers traveling along the dusty byways of life.

God's Heavenly Messengers are universally known today as *angels*. But in a manner of speaking, we're all God's "Heavenly Messengers" here on earth: we all have a story to tell, an experience to relate, a testimony to share; and, like His celestial band of servants, the Creator of the Universe wants each of us to be a Godly emissary of His supernatural love. He wants each of us to follow in the footsteps of His Son Jesus Christ, through a lifestyle of giving, serving, encouraging, and ... sharing the Words of Life!

Couple this truth with the knowledge that God created each of us in His own image—thus placing within our hearts a precious spark of the divine—and it's easy to conclude that ... in a manner of speaking ... we are all God's angels in this life!

If this seems like a novel view of *who* we are—or *should* be—and *what* we're about, it's not! If we truly believe in the God of Abraham, Isaac and Israel, and seek to do His will in all things, then this poetic analogy perfectly reflects both our spiritual identity and our ultimate purpose in this hectic world. Trust us, this "shoe" comes in one size only, but it actually fits everyone!

God, however, desires much more than a clever analogy. He's been calling His people to actually *do* the work of the angels since the beginning of time! We've just missed it. Or should we say, *strayed* a bit from the truth? Fortunately, it's never too late (or too soon) to rediscover a lost truth. And our Lord always manages to gather together His flock, no matter how far we roam!

God is calling His flock to once again embrace its *angelic* role to a world in need. He's actively recruiting these days, looking for faithful servants who are ready to join His band of angels. But do *you* have what it takes?

You do! We all do! But in order to fly with the angels, we'll need to go through some basic training. Call it boot camp for angels—except there's no drill sergeant. And consider this humble little book the official training manual. It won't teach you how to pitch a tent, dig a foxhole, or light a campfire, but it does explain what it takes to develop the "heart of an angel"!

The *heart* of an angel describes the loving, welcoming, and accepting disposition and habits God longs to cultivate in each of us. It's not something that comes naturally, but there are a few *basic* things we can do to facilitate our own growth, all of which we share within. This angelic heart is also strengthened and characterized by a *simple* approach to social interaction which was instituted by God Himself. And while this approach may at first seem an unimportant "side issue," it's anything but. It's the single most important "ministry" of the angels!

The true heart of an angel is distinguished by a lifestyle of *hospitality!*

● STOP! ●

If you think you already know *everything* about Biblical Hospitality, then you probably don't know nearly enough. And if you think the practice of hospitality is not something you're personally called to—no matter what the reasons— then you *need* this book.

To begin with, the practice of hospitality is actually a sacred command for *everyone!* And yet, it's one of the most neglected and misunderstood Biblical concepts today! For instance, it's NOT the same thing as Modern entertaining, and it's NOT for women only!

Hospitality not only characterizes the heart of an angel, but it's also the purest expression of the divine nature and character of the Creator of the Universe! After all, the God of the Bible is first and foremost a *hospitable* God. But when was the last time you heard anyone refer to Him in this way?

With *The Heart of an Angel*, we hope to set the record straight regarding the practice of hospitality, while bringing clarity to several key issues facing our churches and communities.

In the pages that follow, we define God's original concept for social interaction, based on numerous scriptural references, as well as the examples of key Biblical figures. We also explain how the practice of hospitality impacts every area of our lives, and why it's vital to the spiritual, emotional, and physical health of our families, friends, coworkers, and even people we've yet to meet!

We'll dispel several myths surrounding hospitality, which have resulted in the neglect of the practice—to the detriment of both our civil and faith communities. We'll explain how hospitality significantly differs from the art of entertaining, a secular pursuit that's had many unintended and unfortunate consequences on God's people and the world at large.

Along the way, we'll visit with the great Biblical Patriarch Abraham. We'll recount his history-making encounter with the supernatural, and learn how the event changed the destiny of all humankind. And while many know him as "The Father of Faith," we'll show you why he's the icon of yet *another* spiritual attribute, and explain how these attributes work hand-in-hand.

We'll explore the pitfalls of modern entertaining, and then meet two very different "angels" named Martha! We'll learn what God Himself expects from a good host or hostess, and examine the "one thing" that makes God feel truly welcome— in both your heart and home.

We'll explain why "hospitality starts at home," and then tell you how to make that home a refuge of refreshing and restoration, a place where God will show up to work miracles.

We'll even let you in on a few "secrets" only the angels understand!

We hope to inspire and encourage you to fly to new heights, while giving you plenty of new insights to think about. And maybe here and there we'll even be able to supply you with a good laugh! But, more than anything else, we want you to understand what it takes to have the heart of an angel, and why GOD WANTS YOU—and needs you!

Join us in this great endeavor, and learn how you, too, can be a part of God's band of angels!

Tom and Wilma English
New Kent, VA

CHAPTER 1:
TOUCHED BY AN ANGEL!

FOR DECADES the entertainment industry has demonstrated its fascination with angelic beings. Literary thrillers have introduced them into several controversial and pretty far-fetched novels, all to service their doctrinally incorrect plots; and big-budget movies have used every CGI trick in the business to help audiences to "see" these supernatural creatures. But despite all the special effects at their disposal, and despite all the "pseudo-facts" employed by writers, both Hollywood and pop culture have failed at depicting the most vital aspect of God's "secret agents."

Few of these works of fiction have allowed us to catch a glimpse of the heart of an angel! And believe it or not, in real life, it's not that hard to see! In fact, we plan to explore the hidden hearts of angels in the pages that follow, and bring a new perspective to a familiar debate: do angels still operate in the world today? The answer may surprise you!

One iconic piece of pop culture that did manage to capture the true nature of these supernatural beings was the hit television series *Touched by an Angel*, which premiered in 1994, and ran for nine seasons and 211 episodes. Each week the show's two angels, amiably played by Della Reese and Roma Downey, would receive their latest assignment straight from God—which was theologically correct and entirely fitting. After all, as angels, these two special agents are servants of God, sent to earth by Him to help humans with various problems and issues.

In the course of performing their divine duties, these angels would assist people facing difficult times. They might help an alcoholic sober up; find a home for an orphan or a street person; comfort a disabled vet; encourage a dreamer to fulfill a goal; prompt a selfish and materialistic businessman to re-evaluate what's important in life; reunite estranged family members; and, in general, urge their flawed human "assignments" to accept those who are ethnically and socially different, to show compassion for the poor and needy, to forgive people who had wronged them, to reconnect and rebuild relationships, and ultimately to draw closer to God.

By the end of every episode, these wonderful angels faithfully completed their "secret mission." Usually they did so in spite of seemingly impossible odds, and after overcoming incredible obstacles. Nevertheless, they always managed to help their human friends in need—the people God created in His own image—to becoe all that they *could* be!

Throughout the entire run of this encouraging series, one thing remained constant: the angels always made a positive contribution to the lives of the people they encountered, particularly in the area of human relationships. Actually, these agents of God continually left the men, women and children they were assigned better off than when they found them! Hence, the people they encountered knew they'd been "touched by an angel"!

Each of us has the potential to similarly touch the lives of the people we meet. With God's help, we can have a positive impact on friends, family, coworkers ... and even strangers! And we can make a real difference in our homes and communities—*if* we're willing to accept the assignment God wants each and every one of us to accomplish! What's our mission? It may sound a little impossible, but it's not: God simply wants all of us to be His "angels"!

Don't laugh, because the word *angel* comes from the Latin term *angelos*, meaning "messenger"; and God's supernatural agents are precisely that, delivering good tidings and words of encouragement to those in need. But then, don't we *all* have a message to share? In essence, God intends our very lives to send a message to the world. Each of us was created to be His "living letter" to those we meet. (2 Corinthians 3:3) So, in a spiritual sense, we are all messengers. However, the analogy doesn't end here.

People are as unique as their DNA; no two are alike. Furthermore, each of us is the product of our upbringing, our national origin and our ethnicity. Each of us comes from a unique background, with unique experiences. We are all one-of-a-kind masterpieces created by God, and every last one of us can declare with the Psalmist, King David, "Thank you for making me so wonderfully complex! Your workmanship is marvelous!" (Psalm 139:14 NLT)

While we're on the subject, we'll point out that we didn't use the term *race* in the above paragraph. What people generally define as *race* should never differentiate us, and we've personally decided to jettison the word—because we're all members of a single race, the *human* race. We were all created in God's own image, and we're all descended from a single bloodline. (Genesis 1:26) But thank goodness we're not all the same! Our uniqueness and individual "flavor" derive from a variety of cultures, ethnicities and backgrounds. God loves diversity—just take a look at nature and you'll understand this—and when He created the human race He seasoned the world with a wide variety of "flavors"! Or, as Hispanics would say, *¡Sabor!*

Our life experiences, particularly our spiritual journeys, as well as other factors such as education (both formal and informal), gives each of us a distinctive perspective on life. We all have something to share, something special to bring to the table. Each of us has a unique voice and a personal message to deliver. Question is, exactly what type of message are we sending?

Ever hear someone say, "You're sending the wrong message"? Unfortunately, God may have good cause to say the same thing about many of us. At times we *act* and *react* in selfish, self-centered, and shameful ways, saying things we usually regret as soon the words spew from our mouths; but God wants each of us to carry instead a *Godly* message that impacts lives in a way that leaves people feeling as though they were "touched by an angel"!

God wants all the members of His "family" to be *angelic* messengers of love, hope and truth. In essence, He wants us to be the messengers of an ancient and universal practice that has endured the test of time, a sacred charge capable of transforming lives, a divine duty called ... *Oops!* We're getting a little ahead of ourselves.

To become God's "supernatural" messengers, we must first allow God to speak to us and to have free rein in every area of our lives. We must ask Him to give us the heart of an angel!

The heart of an angel can be described with a single word, *Hospitable!* This one word says it all: loving, accepting, welcoming. Hospitable people open their hearts and homes to others; they are sensitive to the needs of those around them; they make room in their lives for the people they meet. Oh yeah, and they continually practice the Biblical (and generally misunderstood) concept of hospitality!

Hospitality is … probably not even close to what you *think* it is! In actuality, it's like an onion! It has numerous layers, multiple aspects and components, and we'll need to "peel" it to fully reveal its heart. We'll start peeling the concept in the pages that follow, but for now, here's a concise definition:

Hospitality is an <u>attitude</u> of the heart (love) expressed through a <u>lifestyle</u> of giving and serving. It's the giving of your time, talents and resources. It's the giving of yourself!

And to be crystal clear, the practice of hospitality is NOT the same as modern entertaining! Although the two share some of the same components, such as food and socializing, and both are connected to celebrations and holidays, the similarities end there. However, even in their similarities, the two concepts are worlds apart. For instance, as we'll later explain, in modern entertaining food plays a vastly different role than in hospitality. Time for a little clarification?

There are numerous *major* differences between these two very different approaches to social interaction. We can't go into all of them here—we thoroughly explore the subject in a forthcoming book—but we *do* discuss most of them in the chapters that follow.

The main irreconcilable difference is that modern entertaining is a *secular pursuit*, rooted in the social values of an increasingly secularized society. It is a pursuit influenced and often motivated by materialism, competition and perfectionism. Modern entertaining has no spiritual component, and hence, there is no eternal significance or consequence to the pursuit.

Hospitality, on the other hand, is a *spiritual practice* which is expressed in a practical physical context. It's rooted in

Godly values, and prompted by the virtues of love, generosity, humility, and service. (Do you remember our definition?) Hospitality has both physical *and* spiritual components, and hence, it produces results that have both a temporal effect as well as *eternal* significance and consequences. We'll discuss this aspect more, in a later chapter.

Furthermore, hospitality—unlike its secular counterpart—is linked to the ministry of angels! During its sacred practice, we reach out and interact with our fellow man, *not* as though we're mere mortal creatures of flesh and blood, but rather with the awareness that we are *spiritual* beings housed in physical bodies.

We do not simply *entertain* (in the modern sense); instead, understanding that people are comprised of spirit, soul, and body, we *minister* to the whole individual. In other words, we not only supply a meal, but we also provide nourishment for the soul, enriching the lives of others with love, encouragement, and the truth about our Lord. We literally become God's messengers in practical and beneficial ways—accomplishing the work of the angels!

The Heart of the Matter

So, those who practice hospitality become God's hands extended, His angels on earth. But there's another side to the coin: those who benefit from our hospitality are also "angels"! After all, *everyone* has a spark of the divine within them, and *everyone* has a special story to tell, an experience to relate, a message to share. Once we understand this, we'll begin to see that *angelic* messengers arrive in a variety of shapes, sizes, colors and backgrounds. And ministering to God's "angels" is one of life's true privileges—a privilege which carries with it many surprises and rewards!

Another major difference between Biblical Hospitality and modern entertaining has to do with purpose. Face it, the very word *entertain* means "to amuse or engage in a distraction." In the secular concept of entertaining, people get together to eat, socialize and enjoy special occasions together, such as birthdays, or activities such as watching a televised sporting event. But how well do people really get to know one another while entertaining (or being "entertained")? Usually not very well, because the emphasis is on the food and activities—not the people assembled.

Besides, activities, crowds, and a lot of commotion, typical situations in most social gatherings, don't provide the best atmosphere for people to share their hearts. Which is why entertaining is usually nothing more than a social nicety of no great importance. Strong words, we know, but read on. We'll more than justify our statement.

Please understand there's absolutely nothing wrong with entertaining (social interaction on a superficial level) because, after all, God created us as *social* beings, who enjoy and need relationships. That's why God gave Adam a companion, and also why He created the institution of marriage—the *first* institution He ever created, and one which remains the basis of the family and the foundation of every civilization since the beginning of time.

God said, "It is not good for the man to be alone. I will make a helper suitable for him." (Genesis 2:18 NIV) "...God created mankind in his own image, in the image of God He created them; male and female He created them." (Genesis 1:27 NIV)

Although modern entertaining certainly has its place in our world, and although it can provide pleasant times, simply enjoying a good meal, engaging in light conversation, and playing a game of bridge are *not* life-changing! So what's lacking? The sense of *purpose* that resides in the heart of an angel!

In contrast to modern entertaining, Biblical Hospitality accomplishes all of the above "good times," but its main purpose is establishing, developing, and nurturing relationships—both with God and our fellow travelers in life. Hospitality goes far beyond hanging out with friends and family; it's about tearing down the social walls that divide us, and building bridges between people who otherwise don't "connect"; it's about arranging those "divine connections" where mutual messengers (angels) are able share, and God is able to restore and repair!

We get the word *hospitality* from the Latin *hospitalis*. We also take our idea of "hospital" from this Latin word, which is wholly appropriate: a hospital is a place of healing and restoration, and that's the true focus of hospitality. When we practice Biblical Hospitality, opening up our hearts and homes to others, we become God's conduits of healing and restoration. Through us, God is able to pour on "the oil and wine" for weary and hurting people. (Just as the Good Samaritan did, in Luke 10:34.) We become His hands extended, and our homes become mini-hospitals, an oasis of rest and refreshing in a "parched and dry" world.

Some might say, "*My* house is my *home!* Not a clinic for troubled people!" No less an authority than the Apostle Paul counters with the commandment: "Share each other's burdens, and in this way obey the law of Christ." (Galatians 6:2 NLT) This verse nicely dovetails into Christ's teachings on servanthood and stewardship, because to accomplish this command, God expects us to use whatever means we have at hand; essentially all the wonderful things He's graciously given us—such as the roofs over our heads! And the bottom line here, is that there's no better avenue for addressing and meeting needs than by practicing hospitality ... in our homes!

John Hagee, Senior Pastor of Cornerstone Church in San Antonio, Texas, once stated, "People are in the middle of a storm. [A test, trial or challenge] Or have just come out of one. Or are going to face one in the future." Hospitality in our homes provides people with a little warmth and shelter in the midst of the storms of life.

Sooner or later, we all go through storms. Having an "angel" on our side helps us to weather them—a hospitable messenger of God's love, hope and acceptance, who opens the door, invites us in, and provides a safe haven; who feeds us with both physical and spiritual food, takes the time to listen, and then lends a helping hand.

The sacred practice of hospitality can provide all the fun and good times of modern entertaining, but unlike its secular counterpart, hospitality is NOT just a "social nicety" of no great importance. Hospitality goes way beyond having a good time, because it serves a higher purpose: there are lives to touch, hearts to mend, needs to meet ... and angels to encounter!

Hospitality is expressing love in a practical way through simple acts of kindness, one person at a time. It can be as significant as the examples we've discussed, but it can also be as simple as a smile, a polite gesture, or a hearty greeting; it can be taking the time to acknowledge an individual with a compliment or an encouraging word; it can even be praying on someone's behalf; and it can take place anywhere and at any time.

Jesus said, "I'm giving you a new commandment ... <u>to love one another</u>. Just as I have loved you, you also should love one another. This is how everyone will know that you are my disciples, if you have love for one another." (John 13:34-35 ISV) The practice of hospitality is how we fulfill this new commandment.

The message of hospitality is: "You are special, and you matter to me *and* God! And you're not alone! I'm here for you, and I welcome you into my life!" Or, as Bobby Schuller frequently states during his weekly *Hour of Power* television ministry, "God loves you—and so do we!" The message of hospitality expresses the heart of an angel!

When we develop the heart of an angel, we can reach the people God strategically sends our way. We can minister to their physical, emotional and spiritual needs, and we can re-fresh, uplift, and encourage their weary souls. And we usually discover that the people to whom we minister tend to help us in return. They are, after all, angels just like us, each with a unique message of their own. Hence, practicing hospitality is never all give and no take. It's another of God's win-win strategies for abundant living!

We have an expression in life, for people who go out of their way to help us or grant us a favor. We often say it when someone watches the kids (or pets) while we're out of town, runs an errand, or takes us on a shopping trip or to a doctor's appointment.

We say it when someone helps us with a difficult move or an elaborate home repair; or when we're feeling overwhelmed and someone helps us to realize everything's going to work out. And we exclaim it whenever there's a problem, such as a flat tire or an overheated radiator, and someone seems to show up just in the nick of time. With relief and gratitude, we proclaim, "You're an angel!"

When we're loving and helpful, welcoming and accepting, our Lord proudly exclaims, "You're an angel!" It's actually another version of "Well done, good and faithful servant!" (Matthew 25:21 ESV) And when we have the heart of an angel, we'll let people know we're in their corner, we'll call and comfort them, we'll send cards and take meals, we'll ladle on a little tender loving care; and our TLC will bring the world that much closer to God! For the heart of an angel, above all else, is hospitable!

Hospitable people are sensitive and considerate. They find ways to help, and then roll up their sleeves. They tend to bring out the best in us, and make us smile. They add value to our lives, and make our days brighter. We enjoy being around them, and when we visit them in their homes, we don't want to leave! We want to hang out with them all the time, because through them we can sense and experience the love of God!

We need these messengers of God's love more than ever today: "angels" who are willing to open their hearts, their homes, and their lives—through the sacred practice of hospitality. More than ever, people are hurting; they're lonely, often fearful, overwhelmed and stressed out. Many of them have lost faith; all of them need a listening ear and a little TLC.

They need someone who can come along beside them, through good times and bad, and bring comfort; they need someone who's a messenger of love, hope and acceptance, someone who can also point them to the Lord, reminding them that "God has said, 'I will never fail you. I will never abandon you.'" (Hebrews 13:5 NLT)

Friends, these hurting, lonely, fearful, overwhelmed and stressed out people need someone like YOU! Someone with the heart of ... hospitality—who'll leave them better off than the way they met them; who'll make them feel as though they were touched by an angel!

CHAPTER 2:

THE *ART* OF AN ANGEL?

WHAT DOES HOSPITALITY have in common with onions? Glad you asked. Before we can answer, though, we must first discuss the wonders of this pseudo-veggie, which belongs to the same family of plants that includes garlic and chives.

The onion is extremely versatile, and to quote a Spanish idiom (translated, of course), it continually shows up in the soup! Not to mention sauces, stews, and chili; omelets, quiches, and souffles; casseroles, vegetable dishes, and all kinds of sandwiches. But sometimes this ensemble player even takes center stage, in crunchy onion rings or as one of those big beautiful flowering onions that feeds everyone at the table!

George Washington used to chow down on a raw one whenever he felt a cold coming on, because onions are chock full of Vitamin C. We're not sure if doing this warded off the cold, but it sure kept Martha away! And way back in 1648, onions were the first thing the Pilgrims planted in the New World. Europeans brought the versatile veggie with them to North America, but they needn't have bothered: Native Americans already knew all about onions, and used them in cooking, medicinal poultices, and dyes!

Athletes in Ancient Greece ate lots of onions, believing they "balanced" the blood. Roman gladiators were rubbed down with onion juice to firm up their muscles, and in the Middle Ages, people could even pay their rent with onions. Doctors also frequently prescribed onions to relieve headaches, coughs, snakebite, and hair loss. And get this, the ancient

Egyptians actually worshipped the onion! They believed its spherical shape and concentric rings symbolized eternal life. Whatever.

Onions are a lot like life, love and relationships: they take many differing forms. There are common onions, available in three colors (yellow onions, red onions, white onions). There are wild onions, spring onions, scallions, and pearl onions. Onions come fresh, frozen, dehydrated, and canned. They can be chopped, pickled, caramelized, minced, and even granulated. All this variety, all this utility, reminds us of the diverseness of relationships, and the many turns that life can take.

And like an onion, life and people have multiple layers. Our experiences in this world are like periodically peeling back another layer of the "onion" to reveal new mysteries, new opportunities, and new lessons. And the same can be said of relationships: in order to truly get to know someone— and to fully understand why we do the strange, idiosyncratic things that we *all* do—we again need to peel back the layers that insulate people from people.

Onions and Life are fascinating and many splendored things! So are onions and people, all of which reminds us of a favorite verse: "How numerous are your works, LORD! You have made them all wisely; the earth is filled with your creations." (Psalm 104:124 ISV)

Without onions, food (and life) would be a little bland! But didn't we promise to compare the onion to hospitality?

Since onions remind us of life, love and relationships, the popular veggie can also represent the Biblical concept of hospitality: God intended the practice of hospitality to be an integral part of LIFE; LOVE is its defining attribute; and RELATIONSHIPS are one of its many benefits! And without hospitality, life would be pretty bland!

But wait, there's more!

Like the onion, hospitality has many layers! At first glance of the outer skin of the concept, one might think it's the same as modern entertaining, just a social nicety of no great importance. But once we begin to peel away the layers (the many facets of hospitality, such as love, service, generosity....) we discover there's more here than meets the eye: fresh layers that reveal a higher purpose than just entertaining; a rich aroma that draws us to greater goals than simply having a good time; and a strong flavor that reminds us of the main mission of hospitality, establishing and nurturing *stronger* relationships with onions. *Uh*, we mean "angels" ... of all kinds!

And yet, we take the concept of hospitality for granted. We think we know all about it, but like the onion, the practice tends to get overlooked. In fact, because very few people go to the trouble of peeling back its layers, hospitality is one of the most neglected and misunderstood concepts in our society today! And when something is misunderstood, inevitably it is soon devalued, de-emphasized, and sometimes even disparaged. Hence, it ceases to be an important part of our lives.

Hospitality was once one of our most important endeavors. Not anymore! Just look around when you leave your home: people no longer acknowledge each other on the street; on the job, coworkers are guarded and distant; and even weekly worshippers may sit in a certain section or pew for years, never mingling, never getting to know the folks on the other side of sanctuary! But the numerous signs of inhospitality go on and on.

One reason for our unwelcoming, unsociable, and entirely unfavorable behavior is that fewer and fewer people are reaching out and, specifically, extending invitations to their homes. That's the best place to get to know one another, but we're often too "busy" to bother. Indeed, even within our faith communities, we tend to pack the Sabbath with so many activities we don't have enough time for one of our most important duties, practicing hospitality. According to Gordon Robertson, host of *The 700 Club*, even the once traditional Sunday dinner, where friends, family—and especially newcomers—bonded by breaking bread, is gradually disappearing.

"Sunday dinners are a time to gather together with family and friends to share the events of our lives and enjoy a wonderful home-cooked meal," states Robertson in his web-series *Sunday Dinners: Cooking with Gordon* (at CBN.com). Robertson is a big proponent of restoring the sacred culinary tradition— and so are we!

Jesus Christ commanded His followers to "Love your neighbor as yourself." (Matthew 22:39 NIV) But how can we *love* our neighbor if we don't first take the time to get to *know* our neighbor? Truthfully, we can't—at least, not in the practical and meaningful way our Lord intends! (And by the way, your "neighbors" are not just the couple next door, or the kids down the street; *neighbor* encompasses all the "angels" we encounter daily.)

Neglecting to practice hospitality, the main objective of which is to build and strengthen relationships—and thus foster unity—has resulted in "anemic" homes, communities and faith congregations. Our relationships, or the lack there of, are greatly suffering. More and more, people are becoming isolated and *insulated.* They hang out with the family of their favorite sitcom, or "interact" with their cyber-friends on social media. None of which is a suitable substitute for developing *real* friends, the kind that will be there for you in both good times and bad.

There is, after all, tremendous wisdom in Proverbs 18:24, "One who has unreliable friends soon comes to ruin, but there is a friend who sticks closer than a brother." (NIV)

Nevertheless, we continue to neglect God's sacred practice. And to add insult to injury, even the word *hospitality* is slowly fading from our social vocabulary. Frequent comments consist of variations of: "I love to entertain"; "They have the perfect house for entertaining"; or "She has a flair for entertaining"!

In TV shows such as HGTV's *Property Brothers* and *House Hunters*, we hear prospective homeowners say things like "We need a big house with a gourmet kitchen, so we can entertain." Once these reality-show participants finally purchase the house, or remodel it, we hear them exclaim "Now we'll be able to entertain!"

Why not say, "Now we can extend hospitality"? Actually, in such cases, we'd rather they didn't! Because what these people have in mind is *not* the Biblical concept initiated by God. And, when "hospitality" *is* used, it's generally in relation to the hospitality industry (hotels and restaurants), which is a sad use of the word. If you think about it, "hospitality industry" is an oxymoron. How can a business ever hope to manufacture and sell love, hope, and acceptance? How can a company be about the "business" of the angels? Hospitality is about building relationships, not making money! Even the Beatles understood this one, when they sang "money can't buy me love."

We don't know about you, but right about now we could really go for a nice crisp onion—*No, wait!*—we mean some *genuine* hospitality!

In the pages that follow, we'll peel back the onion of hospitality to further strip away the misconceptions clinging to it. We'll examine each intricate layer of the sacred practice, revealing its wonders, until we reach the delectable core of the concept, the *truth!* During the process of preparing our "onion," we may bring a tear or two, or make you hungry for some genuine hospitality; but when we're finished, we hope and believe you'll have a better (Biblical) understanding of hospitality and its importance in God's plan for life.

Cutting to the Truth!

The first misconception about hospitality that we'll strip away, is that it's the same thing as modern entertaining. As we stated in Chapter 1, the practice of God's sacred command often shares the same elements with its secular counterpart, such as fun, food, social activities and celebrations, but the similarities between the two *end* there. Hospitality is NOT the same as modern entertaining! Unfortunately, this association continues to confuse the issue and further fuels this *major* misconception of the divine practice.

This one overriding misconception has led to every other erroneous idea about hospitality. Confusing God's Biblical concept with modern entertaining has only led to more misunderstandings, and has created the stumbling block that results in people neglecting the practice of hospitality. It's time to cut the ties that bind us to a secular conceit, and blind us to the truth.

As we previously stated, there are two major differences between these two approaches to social interaction:

Modern entertaining is a secular pursuit with no spiritual component or eternal consequences; and hence, no angels! Hospitality is a spiritual practice with BOTH physical and spiritual components, BOTH temporal and eternal consequences; and hence, it makes room for "angels" of all types (the wide variety of human *messengers* who have a story to tell, an experience to relate, a message to share; and for all followers of the God of the Bible, the main message should be LOVE).

Modern entertaining provides a pleasant occasion with no purpose greater than eating and having a good time; and as such, it is no more than a social nicety of no great importance. Hospitality can provide food and good times, but it serves a *higher* purpose: meeting needs, healing hearts, touching lives, and even encountering angels! Because there are higher stakes involved, and eternal consequences that go beyond having fun, hospitality is NOT just a social nicety that can be neglected if and when we choose.

Let's peel back a little more of the hospitality onion to reveal another big difference between these two vastly different approaches to social activity:

Today, the pursuit of modern entertaining is con-sidered an art. An "art" requires a set of skills and creative ability; and only after years of pursuit, can the artist truly "master" it. Indeed, the art of entertainment requires that one have culinary, creative, organizational, and social skills, as well as a bit of sophistication and an extensive knowledge of proper etiquette. Because there are certain standards the entertaining host must strive to meet, properly executing the art requires a great deal of time, effort and money.

Additionally, the art must be executed in the proper setting. Do you remember those people on the HGTV reality show, who exclaimed—only after buying a new home or remodeling an old kitchen—"*Now* we can entertain"? The art of entertaining is responsible for making people think they need big houses with hardwood floors, the finest furnishings, and custom window treatments; or elaborate designer kitchens filled with granite countertops and state-of-the-art appliances; or formal dining rooms loaded with fine china, glistening silver, and heirloom linens. The motto of the art of entertaining is "Nothing but the best to impress!"

When you're entertaining, preparing and serving a gourmet meal is an absolute must. Each and every dish must be a culinary masterpiece, and regardless of who cooked (or catered) the meal, everyone must be told that all the food was prepared from scratch using only the finest ingredients ... many of which were either raised in the backyard garden or freshly slaughtered from the livestock grazing on the south 40. *Moo!*
Yes, we're exaggerating, but things can really get a bit

elaborate in the art of entertainment. Think "Martha Stewart" and any of a number of her televised holiday specials, where the tablescape is enough to impress the crowned heads of Merry Old England; where the lawn is immaculately manicured, the house newly painted and absolutely spotless; where everything from the food to the music to the family dog (just back from the groomers and on her best behavior) are picture P-E-R-F-E-C-T!

Ooh la la!

Isn't this what comes to mind when you think of entertaining? If so, you're thinking is on the right track, because entertaining is, after all, an art!

Okay, it's time for the practice of hospitality to weigh in. But we're tired of typing, so we'll sum things up by stating:

Hospitality is a matter of the heart, *not* the art!

Unlike modern entertaining, the sacred practice of hospitality is NOT an art, it's a Biblical command. It doesn't get caught up in a lot of *foofoo!* Such trappings can be nice, but they aren't necessary. What is required is your LOVE! And furthermore, when the Apostle Peter said, "Cheerfully share your home with those who need a meal or a place to stay," (1 Peter 4:9 NLT) he didn't qualify his command by saying, "Uh, that is, *if* you have a gorgeous home with a designer kitchen!"

In a more straight-forward translation of this verse, the Apostle puts it this way: "Be hospitable to one another without complaint." (1 Peter 4:9 NASB) The word **be** pretty much rules out having a choice in the matter. He doesn't say "try to be"; it's a command! Period. Done deal. We don't even get to complain about it. The Apostle doesn't give us room for any BUTs. He doesn't command us to be hospitable only *if* we're outgoing "people-persons," or *if* we're gourmet cooks, or *if* we have lots of free time and extra money, or *if* we're highly sophisticated and have our etiquette down pat, or *if* we've mastered the art of entertainment.

Trust us, the Big Fisherman didn't care about any of that stuff. He just wanted us to reach out to our neighbors in genuine hospitality. And while we're on the subject, when this brawny giant of a man, whose hands were thickly calloused from hauling in his fishing nets, commanded us to be hospitable, he was NOT addressing just the womenfolk. Guys, he was also talking 'bout you!

Hey, ladies, stop laughing! Allow us to point out that there *were* women present when the Apostle issued his historic command, and again, Peter never said, "Be hospitable—*if* you're the Martha Stewart-type who's mastered the art of entertaining!

Now's the perfect time to list several aspects of the practice of hospitality (layers of the "onion")—which are absent in the art of entertaining. Hospitality is:

- *a sacred commandment to be obeyed by both men and women*
- *a key qualification for spiritual leadership (both in our churches and in our homes)*
- *a defining characteristic of a Godly man or woman*
- *a practical means of expressing God's love*
- *an effective approach to loving one's "neighbor"*
- *an occasion to make room for "the stranger"*
- *an appointment to encounter angels (any heaven-sent messengers)*
- *a standard practice of reaching out to the poor and needy (the "least" among us)*
- *an instrument for meeting needs and alleviating suffering*
- *an avenue for encouraging and refreshing people*
- *a method of sharing the Good News of Jesus Christ*
- *an antidote for selfishness and isolation*
- *a tool to break down walls and build bridges*
- *a stimulus for true fellowship (or koinónia)*
- *a forum for connecting and building genuine relationships*
- *a catalyst for unifying the family and the Body of Christ*
- *an opportunity to make a positive contribution in the lives of others*
- *a springboard to fun and social interaction*
- *a path to Christian maturity*
- *a way to leave a legacy!*

We'll discuss all of these "layers" in subsequent chapters. For now, however, it should be clear that regardless of our gender, and regardless of whether or not we've mastered the art of entertaining, we're still called to practice hospitality. But to restate the matter, we don't have to be adept in the art, because the Biblical concept of <u>hospitality is NOT a matter of the ART; it's a matter of the HEART.</u>

It's not about gourmet food and designer homes; instead of focusing on such external matters, the sacred practice focuses on the matters of the heart (love, hope, healing). It's not about "perfection" (obsessing over every little detail); it's about relationships.

We'll continue to peel the onion of hospitality in the chapters that follow, further revealing the *heart*—not the *art* of an angel.

ℰℭ

Don't miss out on the conclusion of Tom and Wilma's essential book on hospitality:

THE HEART OF AN ANGEL
BECOMING GOD'S MESSENGERS OF LOVE AND HOSPITALITY TO A WORLD IN NEED!

Available now!
From the back cover:

We've "lost" an important truth that expresses the heart and nature of God, and abandoned a practice that's vital to peace and unity within our homes and communities, as well as the growth of our churches. It's one of the most misunderstood and neglected *Biblical* concepts today, and its inexcusable neglect is keeping us from becoming all God intended!

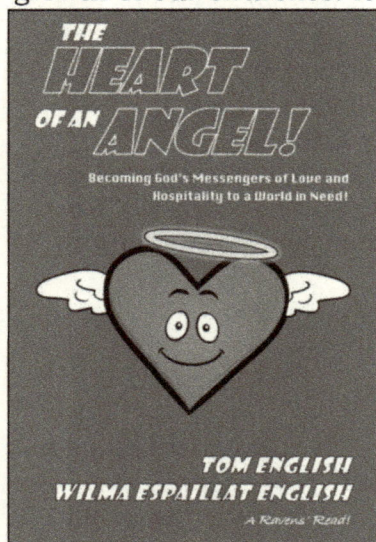

"[Tom and Wilma] ask readers to redefine hospitality by considering it from a biblical sense in this impassioned book....

"Bringing together all the Bible has to say about being hospitable, [this] forceful book will appeal to Christians interested in deeply scriptural reading."

—BookLife
(a division of Publishers Weekly)

(ISBN 978-0996693615 • Softcover • 192 pages • $14.95)

MORE INSPIRATION FROM TOM AND WILMA ENGLISH

ANGEL IN THE KITCHEN: TRUTH & WISDOM INSPIRED BY FOOD, COOKING, KITCHEN TOOLS AND APPLIANCES!

You will believe that a toaster can talk!

Throughout Biblical times, God called upon angelic beings to make special announcements to His people on earth. But God has *many* ways of speaking to us: beyond His Holy Word, we can hear His voice in the roar of the ocean surf, see His wisdom in a blade of grass, and learn valuable lessons from industrious ants and puffy rain clouds. And when it comes to learning about life, love and relationships, God's "heavenly messengers" are everywhere. We can find His "angels" in all walks of life, in books and on television—and even in the kitchen!

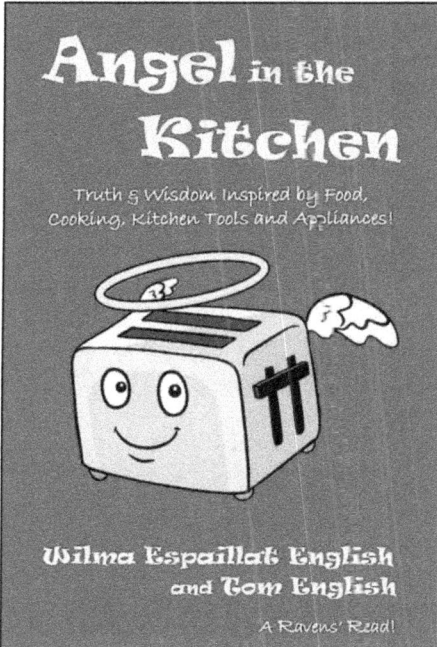

Angel in the

Kitchen

Truth & Wisdom Inspired by Food, Cooking, Kitchen Tools and Appliances!

Wilma Espaillat English and Tom English

A Ravens' Read!

Grab a cup of tea, find a comfy chair, and indulge in this witty collection of thought-provoking articles exploring the sights and sensations found in every home: an eccentric ensemble of kitchen gadgets, appliances and food items —and the important messages they can relate. You'll meet *Luke* and *Nuke*, the twin microwaves, hear the call of the Keurig, and discover why *Fridgey* the refrigerator loves the nightlife. You'll encounter culinary oddballs and weird cookbooks; learn the spiritual significance of Tupperware; and find out what happens when "The Cheese Stands Alone"! These are just a few of the kitchen angels eagerly waiting to greet you within.

Sixty-six of Tom and Wilma's best articles are collected here for your enjoyment. *Bon appétit!*

(ISBN 978-0996693608 • Softcover • 180 pages • $9.95)

SPIRITUAL BOOT CAMP FOR CREATORS & DREAMERS: ENCOURAGEMENT, INSPIRATION & BASIC TRAINING TO HELP YOU ACHIEVE YOUR DREAMS

Are you a creative person? Do you have grand goals and high hopes? Are you chasing a seemingly impossible dream? More importantly, do you have what it takes? To fight fear, failure, and rejection? To weather the storms of life, defeat disappointment, and seize the day? To overcome all of the obstacles on the road to your destiny? To stay the course, no matter how tough it gets, or how long the journey takes?

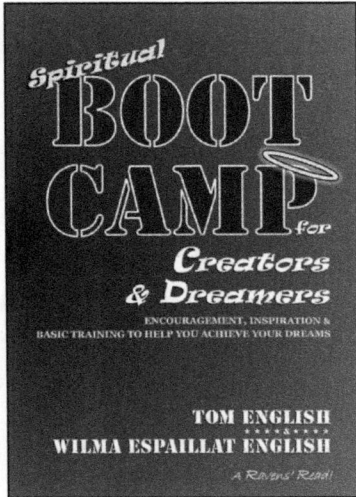

Here you'll receive basic training specifically designed to whip you into shape so you can conquer your dreams and enjoy a victorious life. Tom and Wilma English share their personal battle tactics learned from decades in the trenches—practical strategies reinforced with truths from the Word of God—to encourage and help you to live each day in victory as you continue on the journey to realizing your hopes and dreams!

(ISBN 978-0996693691 • Softcover • 272 pages • $12.95)

"...*The Englishes write with style, clarity, and gracefulness*. They contextualize their advice with real-world examples, while they develop most of their arguments *thoroughly, persuasively, and with scriptural back-up*.

"Ultimately, *while it may look superficially similar to other books in its genre, Spiritual Boot Camp for Creators & Dreamers is uniquely thorough, well-written, persuasive, and inspiring*. ...There are chapters about visualizing goals, managing time, finding and maintaining motivation, learning to pray, and other well-covered advice areas. Fortunately, *their treatment of these common topics is fresh, with engaging, often surprising examples*, such as the 15-page exploration of the story of Captain America. Further, some of the Englishes' advice is original to the authors, such as the chapters suggesting that readers find 'a Barnabas.' Also unique: the Englishes' jokes and their welcome approach to reconciling faith and science."

—The Booklife Prize, 2019

DIET FOR DREAMERS:
INSPIRATION TO FEED YOUR DREAMS, ENCOURAGEMENT TO FOSTER YOUR CREATIVITY!

www.ingramcontent.com/pod-product-compliance
Lightning Source LLC
Chambersburg PA
CBHW031835090426
42741CB00005B/250